Kirtan!

Kirtan!

Chanting as a Spiritual Path

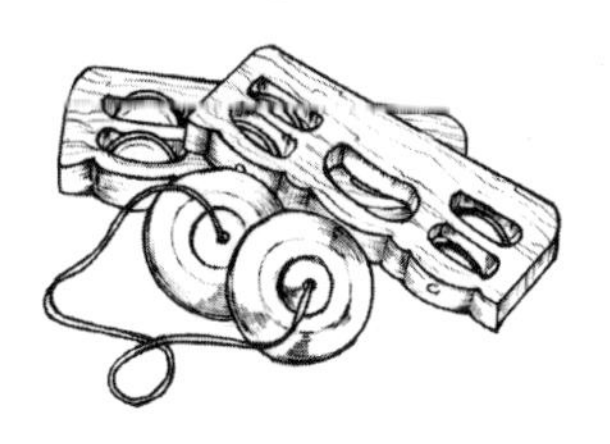

Linda Johnsen
and
Maggie Jacobus

International Publishers
Saint Paul, Minnesota

For information and permissions address:

Yes International Publishers
1317 Summit Avenue, Saint Paul, MN 55105-2602
651-645-6808

www.yespublishers.com.

Photo Credits
Cover photo by Ragani. Photos of Bhagavan Das and Snatam Kaur by Johnathan Brown. Photo of Ragani by Jim Bovin.
All other photos courtesy of the artists.

Library of Congress Cataloging-in-Publication Data

Johnsen, Linda, 1954-
Kirtan! : chanting as a spiritual path / Linda Johnsen and Maggie Jacobus.
p. cm.
ISBN 978-0-936663-43-2 (pbk. : alk. paper)
1. Singers--Biography. 2. New Age musicians--Biography. 3. Yogis--Biography.
4. Singing--Religious aspects. I. Jacobus, Maggie. II. Title
ML400.J64 2007
782.3'45--dc22
2007014829

Contents

Introducing Kirtan 7

Krishna Das 13
Linda Johnsen

Deva Premal 25
Linda Johnsen

Bhagavan Das 37
Linda Johnsen

Snatam Kaur 51
Linda Johnsen

Ragani 63
Linda Johnsen

Jai Uttal 77
Maggie Jacobus

David Stringer 91
Maggie Jacobus

Wah! 105
Maggie Jacobus

Joining In 119

Holy Names 123

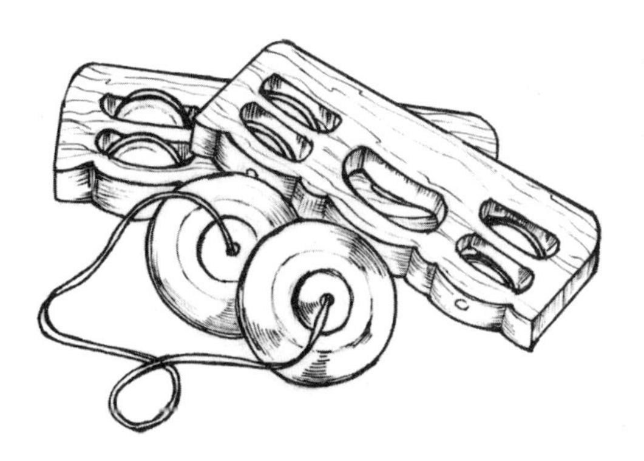

Introducing Kirtan

Kirtan is a spiritual practice that originated in India centuries ago. The word *kirtan* means singing, chanting, and praising the Divine. It's a sacred practice anyone can do; no special training is required. The music does the work for you, carrying you to a state of tremendous joy and mental clarity.

Until recently very few people in the West had ever heard of kirtan. In the late twentieth century a small number of American and European musicians embraced this form of spiritual music, making recordings and going on tours, singing at any venue they could find. Thanks to their sincerity and astonishing talent, around the turn of the millennium the kirtan phenomenon ignited in the Western world. Suddenly kirtan was everywhere: playing at yoga centers, holistic therapy clinics, and medical offices. It was on the radio; it was on satellite TV stations. Soon it was being featured in soundtracks of major motion pictures. Madonna and Cher were including Indian chants in their performances. Kirtan CDs were being considered for Grammy Awards. The magical quality of the music earned it a legion of new fans.

Kirtan is very different from most popular music. It's not concerned with romantic desire or failed relationships or teenage angst. It's about our relationship with spirit, and how to deepen that connection. Though kirtan comes from India it's not denominational. People from any religion, or no religion at all, can participate. Kirtan is the universal language of spirit, the song of the soul.

During a typical kirtan, the kirtan *wallah* (performer) sings a *mantra*, or sacred word, and the audience sings it back. The wallah is not there simply to entertain you, but to lead you to the depths of your own being. The wallah and the audience chant to each other, often singing faster and faster as the chant progresses. A single chant can last from five minutes to forty. You might expect the experience to be boring, but it's not. On the contrary, the music is captivating, even exhilarating. The incessant internal chatter of your thoughts comes to a stop. The problems that weigh at your heart fall away. Sacred sound fills the room, permeates your body, and resonates in the chambers of your mind. You connect deeply with the musicians, with the other participants, and with yourself. The experience is amazingly profound. You leave feeling emotionally refreshed, mentally cleansed, and spiritually energized.

The Un-Concert

The Indian people have always used music to enhance their spiritual life; some of their hymns have been sung for 5000 years. But kirtan as we know it today began five hundred years ago in West Bengal when a beloved Indian saint named Chaitanya Mahaprabhu began chanting in the streets and temples. With his whole heart he would sing out the names and qualities of God in his native language: Govinda ("protector"), Hare ("lord"), Rama ("God"). And everyone around him began to sing back. The movement of passionate devotional chanting inaugurated by Chaitanya still echoes through the subcontinent today.

Because of its Indian roots, many of the mantras used in kirtan are Sanskrit. It's a beautiful language, related to English and most other European languages. Often Western-born people don't know what the Sanskrit mantras mean, though they sense the powerful numinous qualities of the sounds. This is much like the millions of Roman Catholics who, though they're unable to understand Latin, feel the spiritual power when priests chant the old Latin Mass. Today kirtan is sometimes also sung in English, or in other sacred languages like Hebrew, Arabic, or in Punjabi (the language of the Sikhs). But there is undeniably something special about chanting in an incredibly ancient, holy tongue. This frees your mind from having to consider the meaning of the words, and allows you to simply immerse yourself in the living experience of sacred sound.

The main instrument most commonly used in kirtan is the harmonium, a reed apparatus that looks like a cross between a keyboard and an accordion. One hand plays the keyboard while the other pumps the bellows. It's easier to play seated on the ground, so kirtan wallahs and their band members often prefer to sit on the floor. Other classical kirtan instruments include the *tabla* (Indian drums) and *tamboura* (a stringed drone instrument). These days the distinctive East Indian flavor is often complemented with Western instruments such as guitar, flute, violin, or hand cymbals, resulting in a wonderful fusion of cross-cultural music.

But the most important instrument in kirtan is the voice. "There's sacredness in everyone's voice. It's like hearing your own soul," shares Milwaukee-based kirtan wallah Ragani, who leads one of the largest ongoing monthly kirtan events in North America. Your voice comes from within; it is uniquely yours. Unlike an instrument which acts on you, emanating from the outside in, the voice acts internally, emanating from the inside out. When you sing kirtan, you can literally feel the sound resonating inside you, "massaging" your inner organs with sacred mantras.

If you're self-conscious about your vocal ability, kirtan may be the perfect venue for you. Voices blend together, producing a pleasing effect regardless of the vocal talent of the individuals in the crowd. This allows everyone to let loose and participate fully, which is far more important than executing notes perfectly in key.

Many people have been told they don't have a good voice. Kirtan is the ideal place to reclaim your voice, to allow your soul its full expression. By singing out loud you enhance the process for yourself and everyone else. "Kirtan is the people's music," Ragani says. "Everyone creates the music."

That's part of what's so different about kirtan; the audience is inextricably intertwined in the performance. During kirtan everyone there becomes a singer, helps create the experience, and in the process touches the Divine. "In our culture, most of the entertainment is passive. The individual doesn't have an impact on it. Their presence doesn't matter," says Dave Stringer, a kirtan wallah from Los Angeles who tours the globe. "One of the intoxicating things about kirtan is that it's participatory. Your very presence shifts what happens."

Live kirtan is at once both a very personal practice and a dynamic group experience. Singing and breathing together, participants become synchronized. The group melts together, lifting each other up, collectively soaring on the sound current. And then the music stops. That is often the most powerful moment of all. "Kirtan has the outer aspect of singing, but in the space between the sounds when you stop, you'll feel something. And that something is *you*," Ragani explains. "It's not anything that someone is doing to you. It's that energy that is always *within* you that you're feeling."

The Spirit in the Music

According to the yoga masters, the most important spiritual practice of all is meditation. In meditation your senses turn away from the external environment. Your awareness shifts inward, to the center of your being, the inner essence that religions call your immortal soul. You sit motionless in the living presence of the Divine. There are a number of wonderful techniques that can help prepare your body and mind for the inward focus of meditation. Hatha yoga postures are one such method; breathing exercises are another. Kirtan can also serve this special purpose. When the music stops, your mind—already directed toward spiritual dimensions by the mantras—spontaneously enters the meditative state. It's as if you've been delivered directly to the door of the inner world.

Thanks to modern technology, today you can take kirtan with you virtually everywhere you go. You can play kirtan CDs in your home, your car, sometimes even in the your place of business. If you get in the habit of listening to kirtan regularly, rather than the news or other contemporary music you may usually play, the mantras begin to fill your unconscious mind. You'll find yourself chanting to yourself throughout the day. The sacred sounds begin to act as spam blockers for the soul, replacing the often trite or petty thoughts that may clutter the field of your awareness. In this way the practice of kirtan really does become a yogic path, reorienting you toward a more deeply spiritual life.

In this book you'll find information that can help you begin your own kirtan practice. Co-authors Linda Johnsen and Maggie Jacobus interviewed eight of the most respected kirtan wallahs in the Western world today. Their personal stories will help you understand where kirtan comes from, how it produces its magic, and how it can transform your life.

We believe the powerful practice of kirtan can help ignite your spiritual life. The yoga of chanting is an almost effortless way to deepen your experience of the Divine. But now let's turn to the chant masters, the talented singers and musicians who have brought this spiritually invigorating experience to our shores.

Krishna Das

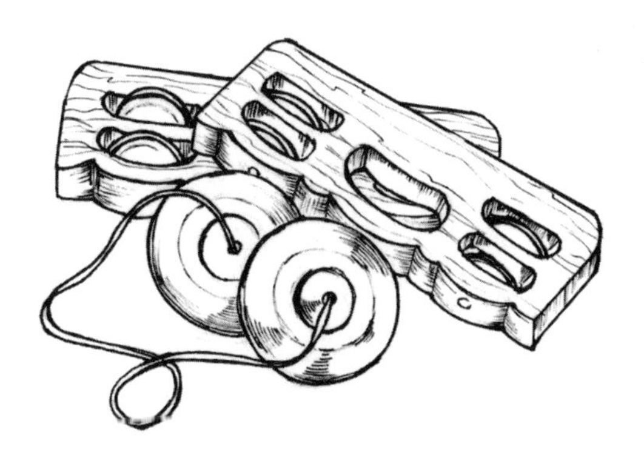

Krishna Das

If there's one artist in the Western world whose name is synonymous with kirtan, it's Krishna Das. His powerful voice propelled kirtan from the background music at local yoga centers onto radio and motion picture soundtracks. He's been featured in *Time* magazine, the *L.A. Times*, and the *Washington Post.* No less an authority than *The New York Times* itself calls him "the chant master of American yoga," while *Yoga Journal* rightly admits he is "the Pavarotti of kirtan." Before Krishna Das, kirtan in the West was an eccentric pleasure. After Krishna Das, it's an international movement.

Today many of us know Krishna Das as the soulful voice providing the soundtrack to our spiritual lives. Since his first solo CD "One Track Heart" debuted in 1995, Krishna Das' passionate rendering of Indian devotional music has introduced tens of thousands of enthusiastic American fans to the spiritual practice of chanting. His CDs, including "Pilgrim Heart" and "Live on Earth (For a Limited Time Only)" have sold over 100,000 copies, phenomenal sales for a New Age artist.

There are any number of kirtan performers who sing from the heart. Krishna Das sings from the gut. When he chants "Om Namah Shivaya," you feel it to the root of your soul. A friend told me her guru asked for a boxful of Krishna Das CDs. "He wanted to distribute them to his devotees there in India. He said, 'Krishna Das is showing us Indians how to sing our own music.'"

How did Krishna Das—a.k.a. Jeffrey Kagel, a disaffected Jew from Queens—wind up a kirtan superstar? Inspired by Ram Dass, author of the 1970 classic *Be Here Now,* Kagel set off for India in September 1970. He lived in the Himalayan foothills for two and a half years as a devotee of Ram Dass' famous guru, Neem Karoli Baba. Maharaji, as disciples called the aging master, was famous for wrapping himself in a blanket and constantly practicing *Ram Nam* (continual chanting of the name of God, "Ram" in Hindi). The twenty-three-year-old American pilgrim "went native," joining the villagers in singing the glories of God, a favorite Hindu pastime. One thing led to another—but I'll let the man tell the rest of the story himself.

I caught up with Krishna Das in Sonoma, California where he'd just led a weekend chanting intensive. I wanted to understand how he'd found a place within himself so deep and powerful that he could sweep crowds by the thousands into altered states of consciousness just by singing simple Sanskrit phrases over and over again. I suspected the source of his power was Maharaji, one of the truly great saints of the twentieth century, and asked him about his spiritual mentor. Krishna Das' eyes brimmed as he recalled his years with the great master.

What was it like being with Neem Karoli Baba?

He did everything from the inside. Outside he would pat you on the head and play with you. The outside was just for hanging out, but the inside was to comfort people. Everyone who came to him was comforted in one way or another. One man came—one of his two oxen had just died. He couldn't plow his land; his family would starve. Maharaji gave him the money for another ox. One old lady came and Maharaji sat her down and he fed her sweets, plate after plate, and she was crying. She said to him, "In my life, no one has ever fed me like this." He fed everybody in every way, all the time. There wasn't anything else he was doing. Beings visible and invisible, in worlds that we couldn't see, all he did was feed them. You need a wife, you got a wife; you need a son, you got a son; your daughter needs to get married, you need a house, you need a job, you need a cure, everybody, everything, on every level, all the levels, he was feeding everyone.

It took a while to get with the program. You have to understand, we came over from America; we wanted to be yogis. He wouldn't buy any of that. We would ask, "Maharaji, how can we know God?" We figured we got the guy here, he knows the answers. "How do we find God?"

"Serve people," he said.

What? It was totally beyond our understanding. We tried again. "How do we raise our kundalini?"

"Feed people."

What? "But Maharaji, how can we be happy?"

"Stop thinking of yourselves."

There's a beautiful story in Ram Dass' book *Miracle of Love.* One of his old local devotees is ragging on him, "Maharaji, you never teach us anything!"

Maharaji ignored him, but he won't stop so finally Maharaji says, "Okay, what are you going to do today?"

"I'll take the bus back to Naini Tal, I'll close up the shop, do some rituals, eat some food and go to sleep."

Maharaji says, "What's the use of teaching? You're not going to do what I say anyway. You've got your lives planned. Beings come already taught by God. Anyone who poses as a teacher does it for the sake of their own ego." He's not talking about saints but about people who want to be known as teachers. He didn't say it was bad, but he was one to call a spade a spade. If you're doing business, you're doing business. It has nothing to do with being a saint.

We just wanted to run our lives through him, and be seen by those loving eyes. We knew that everything happening was freeing us and getting us closer to him, just by being in that vibe. For me the vibe is more present now than it was then in some ways. Most of the time I feel closer to him now than when I was holding on to his foot for dear life because the only thing between him and me was me. And since he's spent the last twenty-five years grinding my head down at the grindstone, there's just less of it around now so I'm closer to him. Your whole life becomes the guru.

The best moments were the sweet, quiet little ones when you'd sit staring at him, seeing all the beauty of the universe wrapped up in that blanket, the glow, the radiance of love everywhere. He'd open his eyes, look at you, break into a big smile and go "Krishna Das!" In every way, in every moment, he would see God, and would see God in us. That was really weird because we didn't see it ourselves. But he saw that all the time. As we go on through life we learn to see ourselves with the eyes of love like he did, and then we can see others with the eyes of love too.

One day a woman visited us from another ashram. He asked her, "What did they teach you there?" At that ashram they teach you *kechari mudra* where you press on your eyeballs and see a light, so she answered, "They taught us to see the light."

He just looked off into space and very quietly, very wistfully he said, "But there's light everywhere!"

We Americans didn't come there for anything other than love, for him. We didn't need jobs. We weren't like some of the Indians, who used him for what they needed to make it through the day, through the horror of their lives. We can't take any credit for that—if we had been born in India we would have done the same thing.

He had a great time with us. Here we were, these crazy people born in another country sitting on the pebbles in the hot sun, singing the name of God. What else would someone like him want to hear anyway?

Why did you leave India?

Maharaji sent me home in March of 1973. In May he turned to one of my guru brothers and asked, "Where is Krishna Das?"

"You sent him back to America."

"*A-cha?* (Oh?) Write him a letter; tell him to come back. I want to hear him sing." He would say to the women there, "Everybody comes here only to talk about worldly things. I'm so tired of this! I want to hear God's name. I want to hear chanting." It was towards the end of his time in the body, the last few months. He wore that body out—it couldn't hold him anymore. But nobody knew that then.

Did you go to see him?

No. The whole time I was in India I was celibate, which to me was essentially taking a vacation from the torture of relationships. I only wanted to be with him. Still after two and a half years, every pore was exploding. He knew that. I also had a fantasy of being a great yogi and going off to the mountains for six months and meditating. But I didn't have the self-discipline. I would have just wasted my time. Of course he knew that too.

One day Maharaji asked, "You think about your father?"

I started to get very scared. I said, "Yeah, it's his birthday, I phoned him today."

"A-cha. You go back to America, you have attachment there."

In retrospect I know I didn't have to go, but I wanted to. I needed to blow off some steam.

My last day in India the visa people were giving Maharaji a hard time, so he wasn't letting the Westerners into the temple. Standing on the platform in front of the temple we could see Maharaji sitting with his back to us. He wouldn't look at us. And then, God bless her forever, this woman named Krishna Priya started singing "Jaya Jagad Ishvara," a song we knew, so we all started singing. He whipped around and shouted, "Come on!" So we all ran in. This was to be my last chance to see him, you understand. It was complete pandemonium, everyone crying and laughing and bowing and fruit flying in all directions. (In India the guru distributes *prasad*, food such as fruit that has been specially blessed, to the devotees who have arrived for a visit.)

I was completely panicked about what to do in America. I hadn't had a pair of pants on in two years. When I spoke English I was like this, "Yes, very nice, just coming!" I had completely immersed myself in India. Finally I just blurted out, "How can I serve you in America?"

He looked as if he just bit a pickle. He said, "You ask about service? Then it's not service. Then I'm telling you what to do. Do what you want!"

Now I had been celibate for almost three years. Can you imagine what I wanted to do? No one had ever told me to do what I wanted. Everybody else said, "*Don't* do what you want." He always said things like that because he knew you're going to do what you want to do anyway. He never created structures that weren't built on reality. Be who you are, it's okay. You want to get married? Get married! You want to go to the jungle? Go to the jungle! Then he leans over to me and says, "So, how will you serve me in America?" As I'm bowing down I hear in my head, "I'll sing to him."

When I got back to the States I had that arrogance people have when their teacher is still in the body. They think they can always go back. I met this woman and we started getting it on. Then the letter arrived saying Maharaji asked me to come back. Because I was getting laid, I didn't want to run back. I thought I'd go in December. He left the body in September.

Whoa!

I was devastated. The betrayal of his love was unbearable. I felt I had totally blown it, the only chance I would ever have.

That moment led to all the karma of my previous days before India coming back on me. I got back on the train of the life that I was leading before I was with him. If you asked me I would say, "I'm a devotee of Neem Karoli Baba," but I was dead inside.

Except for the fact that he is who he is. Eleven years later I went back to India. I'd been doing a lot of self destructive stuff. It was affecting everyone around me, my wife, my kids. I arrived there during Durga Puja and the Indian devotees go, "You've come to sit in the *puja* (religious ritual) with us! Come make the offerings in the place of honor." I just wanted to sleep for a week, but you can't say no. They love you too much.

At the end of the *arati* (candle ritual) one old woman bowed down on the tucket where Maharaji used to sit and she didn't get up. She went into *samadhi* (deep meditative absorption). Forget a knife—I already had a knife in my heart—it was like a spear. I thought, "He's real for these people and I'm so far away from him!" At that moment Siddhi Ma, who was one of his great devotees, called for me. I was thinking, "Why don't they just leave me alone?" But you can't say no. So I got up and followed her into the room where Maharaji spent a lot of time, his inner room. When I walked in the room, he was there. And I fell like a tree hit by lightning. I didn't see him with my eyes, but he was there. I completely disintegrated. I was crying uncontrollably and I could not stop.

I saw every second of my life from the moment I heard he died until that moment, every second like a frame in a movie. I saw everything I had thought and done from a completely clear space. I saw that I'd built a wall around my heart. I was like a stubborn kid and I would not let myself feel him. Every brick of this wall was shame and fear and guilt and anger and self-hatred. But I also saw that he had been with me every second of every day. The wall—what wall? He's in the wall, he's over the wall, there is no wall. He'd never left me for a second, but I wouldn't let myself feel him. And in the next instant I could take the wall down. From that point on I knew that I could live again.

You started singing for Maharaji.

I knew that unless I did that, there were places in my heart that I'd never get to. There was dirt in there, stuff that needed to be opened out. So I started going down to Jivanmukti Yoga Center in New York; it was in August 1994. Every Monday night I would sing. For two years there was nothing more than a few people. It was for free, it was just to do it, to get it out there as an offering.

Chanting breaks down the difference between the inside and

the outside. It's about having a heart that never shuts down, that nothing can shut down.

In India when people retire, they don't want to be a burden to their families, so one day they just disappear. They go to the temple and spend the rest of their lives living there, chanting the name of God. It's a beautiful thing. They suffer a lot I'm sure, but they also are deepening their relationship to God in an incredible way. Look what old people go through here in America, this needle, that operation, this medication, everything but Ram Nam (chanting God's name). They don't get any relief. I'm sure the Indians are hungry a lot and miss their relatives, but they also have an opportunity which almost nobody has in this world, to do nothing but Ram Nam. They turn to God with an intensity that only very good karmas provide.

I hear people trying to chant these days. Some get into too much enjoyment and not enough depth, or too much meditation and not enough expression. Sometimes there's no heart, no juice at all. When Mr. Tiwari, one of Maharaji's devotees, would chant, the walls would shake. It was so intense, so rich, so incredible and so deep. He gave every bit of his being to it. Singing pretty melodies isn't enough. It has to be connected directly to the heart.

You speak of your guru so lovingly. These days guru bashing is more typical.

The naivete of people in loving their guru in the 60s and 70s is no different than the bashing they're doing now. This is the West, we just keep acting out. We expect the saints to be projections of our ideas of perfection, just like we want our lovers to be perfect, and they never are. So what else is new? I think it's a good learning process—people are learning whatever they have to learn, however they can learn it.

The guru is not outside, the guru and God himself are one. One of the things that Maharaji did for me was to free me from the attachment to his physical body. For a long time I didn't know his big form. For me Maharaji was a man who I loved and who I lost.

There was that heaviness left in my heart. When I went back again to India, he took me into himself. I experienced who he is in a different way. I know now he's not the body.

The guru's not different than you are. The guru is the seer, the one looking out of your eyes. That's what I know Maharaji to be. But I would still jump off a cliff if I saw him at the bottom.

I don't put a picture up of Maharaji when I sing because I'm not selling him. You can't buy him. He doesn't want disciples, he doesn't need disciples, and there's nothing to join. Where are you going to go when he's dead? You can't see him, what are you going to do? If I put his picture up, people think that's him and they miss the feeling in the chanting that really is him, his presence, and his sweetness.

Maharaji would lie there and people would come and stuff would happen. There was no edge; he never had to take a position or a posture against anything. It was all clear and open in his sight. He's become the heart of the universe, he's one with that. He has no axes to grind, no karmas that are still blossoming and bringing more stuff. He's here only as a manifestation of compassion.

I need to sing for him and for myself. He made it possible—by grace the situation was created where I could do what I had to do. Grace will allow it to happen but ultimately you have to do it yourself, you have to put one foot in front of the other. You have to become it and the only way you can do that is by using your own muscles. Nobody else can do it for you. The guru can clear the path for you but you have to walk that path; there's no avoiding it. Maharaji used to say, "I've done everything. I just leave the mind to you." Thanks! But he'd done everything. He just leaves the mind which means we have to get in there and iron the damn thing out. It's all done; relax, take it easy, and enjoy. But get in there and do what you have to do to realize it. It's an incredible thing he said.

He threw his blanket over me and it was the sky with all the stars and all the universe wrapped up in it. He showed me that no matter what I think, there's no place outside of that vast presence and that endless love. Then I could just sing. I could really sing.

Deva Premal and Miten

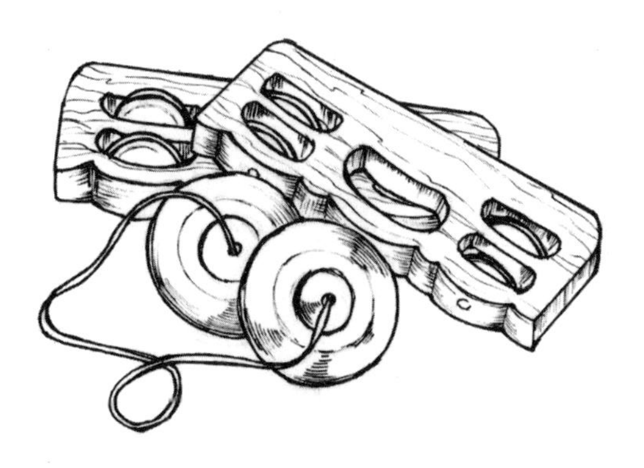

Deva Premal

Some musicians take the world by storm. Deva Premal captured it with the soft breeze of her pure voice. It sounds, for all the world, like the echo of your innermost soul. As Eckhart Tolle (author of the spiritual classic, *The Power of Now*) has said, her music is "a portal into Presence. As you listen, the sacred space that lies beyond the mind emerges naturally and effortlessly."

Deva Premal has been called the Enya of mantra, a spiritual superstar. She has introduced the power of sacred chant to millions across the planet. In fact, her success as a "New Age" artist has been unprecedented. Her latest CD premiered at the #1 position in Amazon.com's New Age CD catalog, and incredibly as the #13 top seller on the mainstream list. Her music has been embraced by leading artists of our time; the version of the Gayatri mantra Cher sang on her last world tour was borrowed from Deva Premal. (Cher has admitted Premal's CDs were the only ones she'd listen to while doing yoga.) The angel-like clarity of Premal's voice, reminiscent of higher worlds, has inspired fans to play her music as their infants were being born and as loved ones were passing away.

Premal was born in Germany to a family that made spiritual life a priority. Her father rose at 3:00 every morning to meditate. He taught his daughter to recite mantras like "Om" and "Ram" when she was a child. She was raised a strict vegetarian and has still never tasted meat.

Music was also an important part of Premal's childhood. Her mother was a musician who encouraged her to learn the piano and violin. Her father, an artist by profession, played drums in his spare time, after he had made them himself! Then when Premal was ten, her mother visited India where she met Osho (Bhagwan Shree Rajneesh), and was captivated by his wisdom and unorthodox insights. She came home and taught Premal how to meditate.

By the time she was fifteen years old, Deva Premal was living in Osho's ashram in India. Eventually she found herself helping to conduct vocal workshops, but only as a backup singer and keyboard player. She was far too shy to take the stage as lead singer.

It was fellow Osho devotee, Miten, who helped Premal find her true voice. At forty-three he was more than twice her age (she was twenty when they met) Miten had made a name for himself as a rock musician playing with bands like Fleetwood Mac and Lou Reed. But his solo career had stalled and his marriage fell apart. Then he too discovered Osho. "I began to meditate. Not only were Bhagwan's words incredible, but his methods were outrageous." Miten moved to Osho's Indian commune. "I was given a new name and a *mala* (prayer beads) and I wore red clothes."

"I began to live my life over again, in a new way. This time, with awareness," Miten recalls. Enter Deva Premal. When he heard her sing, "My jaw dropped. Her voice is so pure, so egoless." He began working with her, and the two became lovers. "I always felt stuck in the rigidity of classical music," Premal confessed in an interview. "It was a great release when Miten introduced me to a world of un-mapped music." It was an auspicious pairing of talent which quickly led to the distinctive Deva Premal sound, a combination of soothing vocal power, quality instrumental backup, and exquisite melodies.

"What I love about these melodies is that they run around

in your head, like a pop song. Only instead of singing some superficial lyric, you're actually subconsciously walking around the supermarket calling on the Divine. And if I can encourage people to remember their divinity as they go about their daily business—well, I feel that's as much as I can do in service to humanity," Premal has admitted.

I interviewed Miten and Premal shortly after yet another sold-out performance in San Francisco.

Twenty years ago, you could only find chanting at a few yoga centers. Now it's entering the mainstream, and chant CDs are being considered for Grammy Awards. Why has the public suddenly opened up to your kind of music?

DEVA PREMAL: People feed what they need when they listen to it. We all realize the way the world goes, the speed and the stress of it all, that this kind of music brings peace and healing. Maybe it's also the packaging, the way the music sounds. The chanting which was around twenty years ago was maybe a bit more—

MITEN: Authentic!

DEVA PREMAL: Authentic yes, but now we make the music also beautiful to listen to for our Western ears.

MITEN: There's a wave that's growing and it's taking people with it. Twenty years ago there weren't so many of us looking. Now more and more people are facing their mortality, and they're actually looking for some deeper meaning for being alive. The search is expanded and it's taking a lot of people who in their youth were more interested in buying into society's dream. Now there's a lot of people in my age cohort, in their fifties, coming to our programs and saying, "I took a different route when I was younger. Now that's done, and I want you to show me where you've been." People are looking for enrichment of their life.

Our generation with its love for rock'n'roll, and succeeding generations with their attraction to disco or country music or hip hop, all turn to music the way we turn to caffeine, to give us a physical lift. You chant sacred mantras and give us a spiritual lift!

MITEN: Chanting is not just excitement-based. When Cher did the Gayatri mantra (on her tour), that was a big indication for both of us that times are changing. Even if she'd just sung the mantra "Om," 15,000 people would have been blessed by their favorite singer. It doesn't really matter who the vehicle is. It's just the sound itself coming out in the arena. Even if it was only show biz it doesn't matter; the mantras can't be compromised.

Your music affects people profoundly. It alters their physical and mental state, almost like a phase change in consciousness. Sometimes it seems as if the music isn't even coming from you, it comes straight from heaven. Where does your music come from?

MITEN: It comes from our meditation.

DEVA PREMAL: I see myself more like a channel. The music comes from something that's beyond the mind and beyond what I can explain or give a name to.

It seems like making divine music is your sadhana, your spiritual practice. Can people use chant music as a form of inner work?

DEVA PREMAL: Totally! It works on many levels. Just singing alone is already healing for the body. Your cells get charged, your whole body becomes vibration when you sing or hum. Then when you use ancient medicinal sounds where every syllable has a certain effect on your energy bodies, you know it's healing on so many levels. Because it's also fun, we don't always see the potency of it. And it's so beautiful to go into silence with it. For me singing is the easiest way to come to a silent space. The silence happens by itself. It's not an effort, not a task.

MITEN: Remember we were around an amazing master for twenty-five years. Whenever Osho spoke it was almost like he had to be pulled down into his body to communicate, he was so far out of it. The silences between the words were so tangible and seductive. I always felt that if I could make music like that, it would be divine. If I could translate his expression of the divine into music, it would be sacred and transforming. The music grew out of being in that atmosphere. We never set out to play in night clubs. The music always came from our spiritual connection and our meditation. I think that's why it affects people so much. It's not show biz. It's not entertainment. It really is about Premal and I connecting in the sacred and sharing that, and owning it and trusting it. Then it can move into other people's hearts.

You stayed at Osho's community in India for years. How did living in India affect you?

MITEN: India is a country all on its own. There's been so many enlightened beings over there, the soil is full of that energy. People there have a totally different way of looking at life. I don't mean superficially, I mean underneath the surface. It's concerned with a deeper spiritual connection.

DEVA PREMAL: We've just been in India again after five years. It was a reminder how India is always ready for miracles. In the West we're so oriented to the outside. In India there is the certainty that an inner world exists, and what it looks like and can give us.

I was at the Maha Kumbha Mela festival in Allahabad in 2001. There were 70-million people gathered in an area the size of San Francisco, all chanting. It was the most sublime experience of my life.

DEVA PREMAL: That must have been amazing!

It was unbelievable, like an ocean of spiritual energy.

MITEN: There's nowhere else on the planet like India.

Speaking of world travel though, you tour as much as ten months a year. Where on earth do you find the energy for that kind of lifestyle?

MITEN: In the mantras. In the music.

DEVA PREMAL: We don't have a concert every two days. We have a pace which suits us. It's something I do with Miten. We are together in a kind of bubble, so we feel always at home wherever we are, just meeting beautiful people. We are always in amazing, incredibly nourishing places. It's the best way for me to live.

MITEN: If it was rock'n'roll it couldn't be done. Every time we play for people we hit such deep relaxation, it sustains us till the next concert. A few concerts ago Premal was feeling fragile. She'd been on antibiotics and was a bit shaky just before the concert, but by the end of the singing she was totally rejuvenated. That's what keeps us going.

What do your Sanskrit names mean?

DEVA PREMAL: Deva Premal means "divine loving." It comes from *prem*, love. Osho gave me that name when I was eleven. Miten is called Prabhu Miten which means "friend of God."

Miten, I was very interested to read about your really wild rock'n'roll background. How do you compare the effects of rock music with chanting?

MITEN: There's this great story about a nun who becomes enlightened carrying water from the well. She was looking into the bucket at the reflection of the full moon. At that moment the bucket split apart and the moon disappeared, and she realized she was looking at a reflection of the moon and not the real moon. At that moment she became enlightened. That's how I see rock music. It knows that the sacred is there, but it never turns around and looks at the real thing. One day I turned around and saw the real moon—which for me was meditation—so I stopped playing music for a year or so. When I first came into Osho's community I just worked and meditated and connected with something deeper. I found I didn't need to write songs to justify my existence, which was basically what I'd been doing as a rock'n'roll musician.

There's so many great rock'n'roll musicians who are totally spiritual. I'm thinking of all the songwriters who turned me on back in the 70s like, of course, Bob Dylan and Joni Mitchell and Jackson Browne and Bruce Springsteen. Leonard Cohen is a great example of someone who can write a song that's so poetic and totally concerned with meditation. He's someone who's really bridged the gap. Still, rock'n'roll is valid in itself because it's a celebration.

Your story is amazing because you wound up on a path that's dramatically different from the road you started on.

MITEN: It's a natural progression. There was a moment when I realized this isn't it, and luckily I was in the right place at the right time, and I got the chance to step on a path that actually brought me home, instead of leading me into a world of excitement or confusion or whatever else.

I have a personal Deva Premal story. About two years ago I was being treated for bone cancer at UCSF Mt. Zion, which is one of the top medical centers in the U.S. When they give you radiation they strap you down so tightly you can't move even a millimeter since they target the tumor and try not to irradiate any other tissue. Then you're rolled into a huge machine that's like a big metal coffin. The first time they put me in, I was so anxious! Then the technicians left the room and started playing your CD "Love is Space" over the loudspeaker. It was fantastic! I was just lying there chanting along with you, "Shivoham, Shivoham."

MITEN: Wherever we go we hear those stories about how the music has affected people. It's humbling because it's so amazing to be contributing to people's lives. Can you imagine?

Is there a chant that's your personal favorite?

DEVA PREMAL: I love them all. The Gayatri is closest to my heart because I've been with it for so long. It transformed my life completely. They always say in India the Gayatri mantra fulfills your wishes. It has given me everything which is here now. The words mean "May all beings on earth reach enlightenment," but as with all mantras the meaning of the Sanskrit words isn't as important as the effect the vibrations have on the body and energy centers.

MITEN: I would say the Gayatri too. The Gayatri is definitely the mainstay of everything we do.

Dr. Richard Petty, the holistic medicine practitioner, said your version of the Gayatri mantra was more than music, it was sound therapy. An awful lot of people would agree. But what about the people who're new to this kind of music? Do you have any specific advice for people who've just been introduced to kirtan?

MITEN: Sing your own song!

DEVA PREMAL: That's basically what I always want to encourage people to do. That was the key to the whole flowering I see happening to myself, finding my song in the mantras. We need to see our own potential and respect it, even if it's something which comes really easily to us. Often we think that we have to work for things if they're going to be worth something. The things which we are blessed with, which are easy, we take for granted. For me my whole life changed when I just did what came naturally.

Music seems to flow from you spontaneously, and people receive it naturally and effortlessly, like breathing.

DEVA PREMAL: I encourage people to sing or even just hum a few minutes every day, or sing along with a CD, because it's so healing and nourishing. Use your voice. Many people have said to us they were told in their childhood they can't sing or they sing off key, so they don't ever sing again. It's amazing how many people are told that. Don't buy into it, and sing anyway. Find joy in singing!

It's funny you should say that because I'm one of those people myself. For years I would go to kirtans and lip sync because I didn't want to spoil the music by singing out loud.

DEVA PREMAL: That's so sad! God doesn't pay attention to how good a singer you are. It's not about that. When you actually hear people who've been told they can't sing, often it turns out they sing totally beautifully. It's usually something one person said to you and it gets struck in your mind and destroys the openness in your voice.

MITEN: That's why kirtan is so great. Anyone can participate, and you get so many chances to contribute. The melody goes round and round and you can hang in there. If you make a mistake you know you're going to get another chance—it just keeps coming.

Take five or ten minutes every morning to sing the mantra Om in your shower, or before you get out of bed. It will set you off on a nice path for the day, and you get used to hearing your voice. The more you do it the more you discover, "Oh yeah, I can hold that note now. I know where that note is, I know where it is in my body, I know where it is in my throat." Then you have a relationship with that note and it becomes your anchor for chanting.

DEVA PREMAL: Or use the time commuting to work in the car when you cannot do anything else. It's a perfect time to put on a CD and sing. Then you come home and you've already meditated for an hour!

Your style is different than the more boisterous music of some other kirtan performers. It's more ethereal, like the tone of vibrating glass. It's a stainless portal that leads to the stillness of pure being.

MITEN: Our music isn't meant just to entertain people. It's born out of meditation and a celebration of life. Our life's work is to create gatherings around the world where people can come together to celebrate and meditate.

How fortunate that in fulfilling your purpose in life, you inspire so many people around the world! I hope you continue on this mission for many years to come.

Bhagavan Das

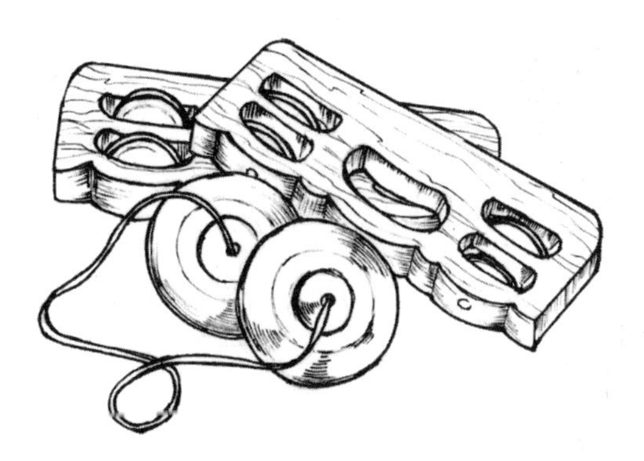

Bhagavan Das

The setting is the Blue Tibetan Inn in Nepal; we're in the heady, drug-stoked era of the late 1960s. "Action!" Cameras roll as ex-Harvard professor and controversial LSD proponent Dr. Richard Alpert first meets Bhagavan Das, a 6'4" blond twenty-three year old from Laguna Beach, California. Bhagavan Das borrows a friend's Land Rover and drives Alpert to meet the famous guru Neem Karoli Baba near Naini Tal in northern India. Cue Neem Karoli, an aging holy man who wanders around northern India half naked, wrapped in a blanket.

Seeing the pair drive up in the expensive Land Rover, Neem Karoli walks over and asks casually, "You came in a big car. You give it to me?"

Bhagavan Das immediately throws himself at Baba's feet. "If you want it you can have it—it's yours!"

"You can't give David's car away!" Alpert sputters indignantly. Everyone around him howls with laughter. New to the sages of India, Alpert is the only person who hasn't realized Neem Karoli is joking—he has no interest in material possessions at all. His only interest is God.

Yes, Hollywood is making a movie about Bhagavan Das' crazy, incredible life. The last time I interviewed Bhagavan Das ("Bhag" to friends)—in Marin in mid-2006—the Hollywood sharks had already bought the rights to his story and were beginning the hunt for an actor to play the 60s icon.

I doubt there are many Americans of my generation who don't know the story, but for those readers who missed the 1960s, let me quickly recap. For Richard Alpert the experience of India was traumatic—and enlightening. Whenever he'd complain about what he was going through, Bhagavan Das would interrupt, "Don't think about the past. Just be here now." Whenever Alpert worried about what might happen next, Bhagavan Das would say, "Don't think about the future. Just be here now."

Richard Alpert (renamed Ram Dass, meaning "servant of God" by his guru) eventually went back to America and wrote a book about his experiences called *Be Here Now.* It became a pop phenomenon, introducing a whole generation to India, yoga, and Eastern spirituality. It also made Bhagavan Das one of the most admired spiritual celebrities of his era.

In 1974 Bhagavan Das recorded one of the first kirtan tapes to appear in the U.S. with a few other Neem Karoli Baba devotees no one had heard of at the time, named Krishna Das and Jai Uttal. That extraordinary tape, called *Swaha,* remains in my estimation one of the most inspired collections of spiritual music ever produced. Since then Bhagavan Das has recorded numerous kirtan CDs, most recently *Now,* and frequently tours the United States and Europe singing passionately to God. His enormously successful autobiography, *It's Here Now–Are You?* is both bawdy and spiritually exhilarating.

Of all the truly great Western-born kirtan singers, Bhagavan Das' story is perhaps the most complex. I asked him to share the tale of his journey from spiritual illumination in the Himalayan foothills to complete disillusionment with spiritual life at a used car dealership in Santa Cruz—and how he ultimately found his way back to the loving embrace of his guru.

I'm curious how an American boy from Laguna Beach wound up a sadhu *(wandering ascetic) in India. In the mid-1960s most of us were just beginning to learn about yoga and the saints from India; you were already over there, "apprenticed" to one of the great saints of our time. How did that happen?*

I truly don't know—I was simply led. I followed the bread crumbs out of the forest and they led to Neem Karoli Baba. When he first saw me, he grabbed me and put me under his blanket. I was brought to him by sincere devotion. As Anandamayi Ma (the much-loved 20th century Bengali saint) says, "Sincere devotion to God is the way to God." You want to know the way? Really want it! That's the way. How I got started wanting it, I don't know, except that I always felt like a stranger in a strange land. I never felt quite at home in the world. When my mother would pick me up from the beach and bring me back to Taco Bell, it was always a major upset. Looking at the world through the dirty windows in the car, I realized something was wrong.

What turned your sights to India?

I knew I had to get out of America; I didn't know much of anything else. I sold my guitar and went to Europe. I ended up in Greece with all these avant garde poets. A few of them had come back from India and were talking of saints, holy men, lots of hashish, and houseboats in Kashmir. I was like, "I've got to go to India!"

But seriously, here's what really happened. One night I was sitting at a friend's house on the island of Hydra and he had a picture of Hanuman in his room. It was a big, giant monkey meditating with a halo around his head. Something about it really struck me. I knew "Om" from my reading—I knew it was the name of God. I went out and sat on the ledge of his porch and started chanting Om at the full moon. I got so out of my body Om-ing that I fell off the porch onto my face! I knew when I came back into my body that I had to go to India. This was 1964. I set off hitchhiking, and got to India three months later.

When you got to India, how long did Maharaji (Neem Karoli Baba) let you fool around till he brought you into his presence?

Maharaji let me cook in the fire of India, which is a fierce fire, for a good, solid year. I was in such culture shock when I landed in India, that I didn't eat for six months. Coming from a middle class American white suburban background into major third world chaos, what do you do? You freak!

I got deathly sick the moment I got to India. I had a high fever and was delirious. A Sikh woman with a big nose ring took me in as her child. There was no place in her mind that I wasn't her son, so she sat for hours mopping my head and healing me. She loved me like I had never been loved before by my own mother. It shattered my conceptual mind. It didn't make sense. I didn't know these people. Why did they seem to know me?

Then someone offered me a room in his house, which he called his Temple of Silence. He locked me in this room. There was a little toilet in the corner and a fan and a cot. It was a dark room with light filtering in through the top windows, and there was a hole in the bottom of the door where he slid food in. I stayed in there alone for two weeks. I started meditating. I understood that what I was looking for was inside of me, and started going within.

Two weeks later the doors of this room opened up and I walked out into the sunlight and there were fifty people standing there. They put flowers around me and they all touched my feet! I stood there and went, "Wow! This is great! Now I know what I want to be in life. I'm going to be a saint, and I'm in saint school!" They were treating me like I was a holy person. Something clicked inside of me and I went, "Oh, I'm a holy man. Well, now I have to follow through." There was this complete sense of peace. I was eighteen.

I got on the train and rode through the dreamscape of India. I felt totally at home now. I really liked being barefoot and wearing a *dhoti* (a sheet of fabric wrapped around the thighs and loins). I think it's really comfortable, like hanging out in your underwear all the time. I thought, "I like this country. Everyone's hanging out in their underwear, just sitting in the street."

I went to Rishikesh and became a fervent meditator. All I wanted to do was meditate and go inward and go inward and go inward. I ended up living with a famous *siddha* (highly advanced yogi) named Tatwalla Baba. He said, "Here's your cave," and I thought, "This is so cool, man! I get a cave, all the perks, they bring me food, people respect me. I like this!" I was so happy. And I got to just go in, to have this adventure inside. My job was just to stay inward. And everything external was taken care of. That's basically what happened. I would sleep three hours and meditate all day and night. I just loved it.

Then one day a swami from Dehra Dun took me into the mountains. He said, "There's a very famous saint I want to see." We stopped the car and there was Neem Karoli Baba. He was a little old man in a blanket with a twinkle in his eye. The moment I saw him, my heart just blew open. It was like someone kicked the door open. He blessed me and I had never felt so loved in my life. He walked in the room and the whole room disappeared—there was nothing there but him.

That's how I met him. He put me under his blanket and I cried continually for two weeks. I never cried so much in my whole life. I'd cry in my sleep. My clothes would be soaked, the bed was soaked. I couldn't stop thinking of him. I'm serious. I would just sit like this and tears would fall. I wasn't sad, I wasn't happy. I went to one of his devotees and asked, "What's going on?" He said, "Maharaji has opened your heart to God." So that's what happened to me.

He kept me with him, near his body, twenty-four hours a day for six months. What he was doing was repeating God's name twenty-four hours a day. All the time. He never missed a beat. He could talk like I'm talking to you, and was constantly repeating God's name under his breath—never, ever stopping. He said, "In Kali Yuga (the current era of spiritual darkness), take the name of God continually and you'll attain everything." My experience is that this is so. But people don't have faith. They can't believe it's that simple.

Ninety-nine percent of the people who came to my guru wanted to watch him do miracles. They wanted him to get them a husband, get them a wife, get them money, help them pass the test in school, "I'm sick, my dad's sick, my mother's sick." Think of how he must have felt! He had God! He has got God, he talks to God all day long, night and day. Nobody wants God!

I spent seven years in India under his blanket. That's the way I see it. I tried to run away many times, because I was young, you know what I mean? I was an American. "He's not going to tell me what to do! I'll do what I want to do!" But I never could leave his blanket.

Where did you go when you ran away?

I traveled all over India. At first I had a vow of never staying anywhere more than three days in order to not become attached to any one place. So I lived on the road. Wherever I'd go, people always greeted me with open arms. Because I was holding the state my guru had given me, I had real spiritual authority, *adhikara.* It was really great because the village people kept me in line, because the only way I could continue to eat was to be a real sadhu. I had this social mirror where I said, "I am a yogi," and villagers made me be a real yogi! You want to eat? You have to keep the inward state. But we cannot hold that inward space without the blessings of the saints. This is the key, okay?

For a brief period during your adventures, you wound up shuttling a fellow named Richard Alpert around. Did you have any inkling at that time that Richard Alpert would make you a world famous figure?

None whatsoever. I was just trying to help him out. He was so sincere, he was really trying to find something beyond LSD. I just did my best to help him out.

Why did you leave India?

My guru pulled my ticket. The parking meter said "Expired." He actually told me to go back to America years before I met Richard Alpert, but I said, "No, I won't go!" and ran off. I went back to the Himalayas and lived in Nepal a couple of years. That's where I met Ram Dass and took him to meet my guru.

Ram Dass blew the whistle on Neem Karoli Baba, and brought thousands of Westerners to see him. The whole thing was Maharaji's divine play. He decided to come to America. He came to America in *Be Here Now.* That book is now in its thirty-seventh printing; it's been in every bookstore in America. It has nothing to do with Ram Dass. It has nothing to do with me. It's all Maharaji's doing.

What happened when you came back here? You vanished! We didn't hear about Bhagavan Das for twenty years.

When I came back to America I was in an incredible space. In other words, I had my *sadhana* (spiritual practice) going. But through hanging out with the wrong people and indulging in *siddhis* (psychic powers) I left it. At first I toured and was a spiritual celebrity. I was on stage before thousands of people, and I named babies and blessed people, and people fell at my feet, and inside I was really unhappy. I lived like a king. I had a chauffeur, I had multimillionaire patrons, and lived with movie stars. I had the finest of everything. I had siddhis: I thought it and it happened. I looked at the girl, she was in my bed

I missed my guru and the village people in India, but I was caught in the *maya* (illusion). I couldn't keep the saint space going because I didn't have a support system. I was still a kid, and I'm a guru at twenty-five? You know, sitting on my tiger skin in a Manhattan townhouse with all these high-powered, famous people around me? I had money, sex, power. So I got to play with that. I guess I wanted it. I got to play out my power trip, which I see as what I attained from going after the siddhis. I got the siddhis and then the siddhis got me.

It's very, very important to realize you cannot play with the *Shakti* (divine power). If you play with her, she will play with you, and she will win, because she is the Divine Mother. She's all planes of consciousness, she is all the siddhis, she's all desire, she is the world, she is everything in all forms. She owns the world, she owns it all. How can you control her?

There are only two ways to control Shakti. The first is to become like a little baby. An infant is helpless and completely pure so we pick him up and take care of him. In the same way, Mother will take care of you if you can be that pure.

The other way is to become a corpse. I was on the corpse path. You meditate, go inside, you die, and you become *Shiva* (pure awareness), and then Mother stops dancing. Stops dancing means she stops the play of the *gunas* (cosmic forces) and you're able to go into samadhi, a very deep state of meditation.

But if you want name, if you want fame, if you want money, if you want occult powers, if you want sex: you can have it all. Mother will give you as much as you want. There are many rooms in her house. When you don't want to play with her anymore, and you want to be taken into her arms and really surrender to her, she will take you, but only then, when there's no more left of your ego than a corpse.

There's no end to this. You cannot stop your sadhana. I had attained but I stopped, and that's when I lost everything. Spiritual life is not a once-and-for-all game. It's an ongoing process. My guru had attained, but he never for one moment stopped repeating, "Ram, Ram, Ram, Ram, Ram" (a name of God).

You spent three years as a spiritual high roller. What happened then?

I was at the party for three years, then I got sick of the party. I just wanted to be home with my children. So I did that. I rejoined the world and lived as a businessman. I sold used cars in Santa Cruz. And then I moved into direct sales for twenty years. I probably averaged $3,000 to $5,000 every month. Fancy suits, expensive cars—I did the whole trip.

Were you able to maintain your spiritual center during this period?

I lost it completely. It was a gradual process. I didn't have *satsang* (spiritual companionship). You must have good company. You have to hang out with pure people, with people who really are on the path, who are sincere, and who elevate your mind.

Then suddenly, a few years ago, the light came back on. You were Bhagavan Das again.

A friend took me to see Ammachi (the famous "hugging saint.") She looked in my eyes and said, "Ma, Ma, Ma." She was repeating the name of the Divine Mother. I hadn't been in the presence of anyone with that level of devotion since I left India. I sat down and went into deep meditation for three hours. For the first time in years, Maharaji came to me in a vision. He said, "Go! Sing God's name! Sing, sing, sing!" So that's what I'm doing. From that moment everything has been working again. But this time I'm being more cautious, watching who I connect with. I spend as much time as I can with saints.

Maharaji sent me back to America to inspire people to get their practice going because that's what going to transform them. My trip is that I'm a real human being, and if others can learn from my experiences, positive and negative, then everything that's happened to me has happened for a reason.

You're back in your dhoti, poor as the proverbial church mouse, wearing your rudrasha *beads (prayer beads), playing your* ektar *(one stringed instrument), and singing traditional Indian* bhajans *(hymns) as well as good old-time Gospel songs, even Bob Dylan tunes about spiritual life, songs from all traditions that turn our minds to God. I've attended several of your kirtans, and after every one people come out gasping, "That was incredible! When Bhagavan Das sings, I'm lifted to another state!"*

Nada Yoga (the yoga of sound) is using music to return to who you really are, to your essence. It focuses devotion through sound to transport us out of our intellects into our hearts. The mind mesh captures us. We get lost in concepts, and we imagine that because we read something or we thought about it, it was an actual experience. But it's not the real thing.

Nada Yoga means tuning in to the inner *nada*, the inner Shakti. We use the external singing and music as the tuning mechanism. When the music stops we enter the silence. Go into it because it echoes into the inner nada and the inner nada will take you to God. It's the sound of Krishna's flute, it's the sound of Shiva's drum. It's the inner Om. That's what I heard in Greece when I fell off the porch. I sounded it, Om, for an hour, and when I stopped I heard it inside and it put me into a samadhi, a state of oneness, and I lost body consciousness.

Use the voice to return to the source. Use sound as the object of meditation. The Divine Mother is the sound. She's the nada. My whole sadhana has always been this. I would sit alone in my little hut in the Himayalas and chant God's name with fervor and intensity, and then I would go into a thoughtless state for an hour, two hours, four hours, however long I was blessed to be able to be there. The moment thoughts came back in, I'd start chanting again, bring the energy back up.

It's so simple. And so hard. Ramakrishna said, "In the Kali Yuga, if you cry to the Mother with all your heart, she will come." My guru said, "Forget about tantric yoga, forget about raising your kundalini. Take the name of God, and kundalini will rise. Repeat 'Ram, Ram, Ram,' and everything will be accomplished."

You need to keep working. It's not a free ride. And be careful if you think you've attained because you can lose it. I mean, look what happened to me. Keep your commitment and keep your practice going. It's really important. Keep the purity, keep satsang happening. Keep your prayers going, keep that inner fire alive. We need to keep this process going throughout our lives, all of us, because we're temples of the divine here in these bodies. True spirituality is experiencing the sacred nature of all life and of every moment. Be wholly present—a holy presence—in every single moment, wherever you are. Just be here now.

I believe we've reached the end of materialism and consumerism. People are very unhappy. It's the name of God everyone is hungry for; they just don't know it. Americans worship Shakti: money, fame, power, all things to do with energy. The energy of the divine names is very, very powerful. It's transcendentally powerful. The whole civilization of India is built on mantra. Southern India is completely built on "Om Namah Shivaya," northern India on "Ram." That vibration brings people out of the mind's web. It brings them closer to their hearts. It creates a state of bliss and becomes a vehicle to carry them into a deeper sense of what's really happening in reality, which is love.

The power you feel during the kirtan, it's not my voice. It's *her* voice. Sarasvati (Shakti as the goddess of music) manifests and the whole room becomes one with her. I'm listening to me singing like I was sitting in the front row. I'm not doing it, it's just happening. It just blows my mind.

Kirtan means "to cut." To do kirtan is to cut through discursive thought and subconscious gossip. It means to cut through conflicting emotions and conceptualizing. The name Kali (Shakti as the goddess destruction) means "to take away darkness." The name Chandi (Shakti as a warrior goddess) means "she who eats thought." How does she eat thought? With mantra. *Man* means "the mind," *tra* means "to protect." A mantra is the force that protects the mind. It is a form of the Divine Mother. This is why we're singing the mantras.

The great strength in Islam is the holy name Allah. Five times a day you hit the deck and cry "Allah! Allah! Allah!" That's a powerful practice! And it's simple. Same with the Hindus, "Ram, Ram, Ram," and the Tibetan Buddhists, "Om Mane Padme Hum." The mantra is the power that dissolves the mind so that one can then find the truth of the heart which is pure devotion.

The idea of *bhakti* (spiritual devotion) is very simple. We think God is so far away and so big, how can we ever get to God? But if you make yourself beautiful and pure, God will come to you. How can we do that? We all love to sing so we go to a kirtan. Outwardly it's the Sing Along Club. It appears to be a concert or a show but it's really the deepest inner temple. We use the energy of our voice to transcend the energy of our mind. And God comes and listens to us sing. How do you come to be in the presence of God? By remembering God. Divine thoughts bring you to divinity.

We're in a major turning of the wheel right now. Times are really cataclysmic. We can no longer afford to shop as a way to take our minds off our primal angst of existence. We're living in a powerful transformational time. I feel that what's coming down on this planet ecologically, spiritually, materially, economically, is going to shake our world to its roots. But because the darkness is so deep, the light is even more brilliant. So all those who really do serious sadhana, spiritual practice, will get huge amounts of benefit right now.

We've been dumping on Mother Earth big time. The shit has piled up and a major enema is required. It's coming in the form of Katrina, hurricanes, and earthquakes. It's important to get down on your knees and pray for real. Keep the mantra going. Sing till your heart splits open. Whatever your path is, now is the time to go for it.

What's ahead for Bhagavan Das?

I am trying, more and more, to be the Divine Mother's child. When there's less of me and more of her, there's greater blessing. It's the great disappearing act.

We're the same person, all of us. Everybody is us. You experience that in kirtan, singing together. When you chant you feel it's all you. That's what people need to experience. We're all in God together.

Snatam Kaur

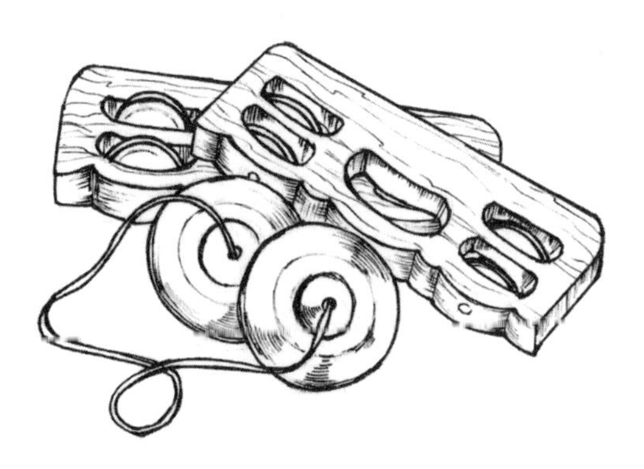

Snatam Kaur

Everyone is on their feet, arms in the air, dancing and singing as Indian music fills the night. No, it's not a clip from a Bollywood movie; it's Snatam Kaur Khalsa teaching several hundred Californians here in a Sacramento auditorium how to *bhangara*, swaying and swirling in the distinctive Punjabi folk dance style. She shows us how to rock from one foot to the other and snap our heads from side to side like we're on a film set in Bombay.

Laughing and relaxed, the audience settles back into the chairs. Now comes the part of the program most of us came for: the sacred chant. The musicians are dressed in traditional Sikh garb, but there's nothing Indian about their instruments: an electric guitar, a keyboard, and a drum set. Snatam uncovers a harmonium as she explains, "Kirtan is the soul and life of the Sikh tradition. It's the main way Sikhs express their devotion to God, and share with each other the joy of singing God's praises. There's a real energy that happens when a community gathers to sing together. It's a part of our daily practice to sing."

Snatam travels the world introducing people to the universe of Sikh chants. The Western arrangements and instrumentation make the songs easily accessible to the widest possible audience, and have helped turn her CDs into one top seller after another on the New Age charts. Her album *Shanti* was so well received it was even considered for a Grammy nomination. And her recent European tour attracted enormous audiences. Thousands showed up for her programs.

"What happens in Vegas, stays in Vegas," Snatam continues, smiling. "What we're doing tonight is the opposite. We're going to create peace and love here in this room, then we're going to send it out to everyone in the world."

Snatam (pronounced *sun-ah-tum*) was born in Colorado to American devotees of Yogi Bhajan (1929-2004), creator of the 3HO Foundation (the three H's are "happy, healthy, holy"). Yogi Bhajan was arguably the most influential Sikh in American history, helping promote the Sikh tradition in the West and introducing students here to Kundalini Yoga. One day when Snatam was eighteen, Yogi Bhajan heard her sing. Her voice was so beautiful, it moved him to tears. He urged her to continue his work through the medium of her music. She has been singing and teaching Sikh methods of yoga ever since.

In your childhood you lived for a short time in Amritsar, India, which is ground zero for Sikhism.

Sikhs love to sing together, and share food with each other and with anyone else who comes. At the Golden Temple in Amritsar 10,000 people are served every single day. Both Sikhs and non-Sikhs come to partake of the kirtan, to be in the holy environment, and then to eat.

I've been to India four times in my life. The first time I was six, really young, and was embraced by Sikhs there. My mother, who was a musician and kirtan singer, began to study with a man named Bai Hari Singh. We started going over to his house, and I was like their white grandchild. Bai Hari Singh had played at the Golden

Temple for sixty years. He was an incredibly accomplished musician and has passed his skills on to his children and grandchildren. I was always sitting in their laps getting my cheeks pinched. I returned to India in my teen years and requested permission to study with Bai Hari Singh because of my longing to learn more on my own.

My experience in India was that people naturally live a more devotional life. They're more inclined to have faith in God and to live in spiritual terms. In physical terms it might take you an entire day to fax a document, and the lights go off in the middle of dinner. But there's a lifestyle of spirituality. Every morning at the Golden Temple there is early morning kirtan, and continuous spiritual activity all day long till very late at night. I was humbled by the way people lived, by what it meant to be spiritual in India.

When I came back to the United States I had to make huge adjustments, it was so different. But that sense of touching upon spirituality on a regular basis was an incredible gift I brought back with me.

You and your family lived your Sikh faith here in America for most of your life. Who was your guru here?

Yogi Bhajan is my spiritual teacher. He brought over the teachings of Kundalini Yoga to the West. Many people became teachers under his care. He never went out trying to make anybody a Sikh but some, including my parents, became Sikh because of his love and inspirational spirit.

But Sikhism is actually centered around the Shabad Guru. Shabad is the sacred energy or recitation of sound, and guru means the living teacher. For Sikhs, our living guru exists within the sacred words of our tradition. As part of our daily practice we take a *hukam* or sacred divine reading from the *Siri Guru Granth Sahib*, which is a collection of writings from enlightened teachers and sages in India. It includes the Sikh gurus, but also incorporates saints from other traditions. These sacred poems were originally sung in specific notes, exactly as the words were originally recited by the gurus.

So our tradition is passed down through singing and recitation. Every morning we pick one poem or sacred reading from the Guru *(Siri Guru Granth Sahib)* which serves as the guiding light for the day. I was taught at a very young age that if you want the answer to any question, if you want to find peace or solace or inspiration, then go to the Guru. Yogi Bhajan was always very clear on this point. He said, "Don't bow to me. That would be ridiculous because I bow to the Shabad Guru, the *Siri Guru Granth Sahib.*" As I grew up I learned to recite shabads for specific things, or I'd hear someone else sing a shabad and be inspired. This energy was alive and would actually come to me and give me healing, or give me a message that I needed to do something in my life.

The living presence of the Guru through sound is our foundation. We really feel the Shabad Guru has blessed our lives, and when we sing it, it affects our physical body and our environment. The reason we practice it every day is so we can create within us that resonance of peace, and then go out into the world with that resonance still supporting our words, and still in our thoughts, and still creating the light around us, because those sacred words are our living master on this planet.

This is incredible! You're saying in your tradition the actual sound current, the songs of wisdom and devotion sung by great sages in ages past, is the living, blessing force that's manifesting to you today as your Guru. Your Guru is not any particular person alive now, but a transmission, a stream of wisdom energy that's been passed down through the centuries by living men and women as they chant the words first spoken by enlightened masters long ago. Your scripture, the songs of the Siri Guru Granth Sahib, *is actually alive, it's a living force that guides and heals and illumines your life. So Yogi Bhajan was your spiritual teacher but not your guru. The Guru of all Sikhs is the Shabad, the sound current. You tap into it by chanting it till your whole being resonates with its blessing power. What a concept! I am totally blown away.*

I love to talk about this. The practice of Shabad Guru came from the original recitation of the original guru who spoke or sang those words. Guru Nanak, who was the first guru of the Sikhs (1469-1539 A.D.), would sit under a tree and be inspired, and these beautiful words came through him, and he sang them. He was a human being channeling those words. The words were recorded and now they're recited in the exact same way he first sang them. Hundreds of years later his disciples can tap into that same energy and imbibe the living Guru within their own being by reciting those same words on the same frequency in the same tone. It's such an incredible experience when you realize hundreds of years from now this living sound current will continue on its own as a transmission of energy.

There's an actual yogic and scientific effect that happens when you sit with a straight spine and chant these words. The energy rises through the spinal cord to the top of the head and there the tenth gate opens, which is the connection with the infinite. Also the tip of the tongue touches the roof of the mouth and this stimulates the glandular system to secrete, giving you an experience of well being in your physical body. These words are exact in their power and potency. The way you vibrate your tongue at the roof of the mouth helps create these very incredible experiences.

Now that I understand a little better what the Shabad Guru is, I see that people like you are the living physical embodiment of it. The tradition itself is literally being carried by these kirtan singers.

There's a quote in the *Siri Guru Granth Sahib* which says "the Guru is the song of God." And you carry that song of God with you; you carry the living Guru with you all the time.

What did you mean earlier by the word hukam*?*

Hukam means "divine command." In the Sikh tradition when you want to obtain a hukam you take the *Siri Guru Granth Sahib*, our sacred body of texts, and open it up and wherever your eye lands, it's where you're supposed to land. When the Guru speaks it's called a command, not a suggestion or advice. The beautiful thing is that the main message of all the commands is to remember God's name. That's one of the chief responsibilities of a Sikh, to remember God's name and help others do so as well. That's what we do in kirtan.

You said Guru Nanak was channeling the sound current. What then is the source of the sound current Guru Nanak tapped into?

The first words of Guru Nanak were *Ek Ong Kaar. Ek* means "one," *Ong* is "the creative infinite flow," and *Kaar* means "the Creator." So there is one Creator and Sat Nam, "Truth is that Creator's name." So the original source is God.

The Sikh gurus say you can't describe God. God is so attainable and yet unattainable, and God is totally with us all the time. For those who feel God is close by, God *is* close by. This infinite flow of energy that Guru Nanak tapped into—and that he created a scientific language and technology for—people on their own can tap into as well. It's not only some sages in the mountains that can achieve enlightenment, but people who live and work and have families and are serving in the world. For them enlightenment is attainable also.

I met Yogi Bhajan shortly after he first came to the United States. I remember him being fantastically charismatic and very dynamic.

I knew him since I was a baby. He was an incredible teacher for me. I talked to him about everything. He was very accessible to me, which was an incredible blessing. Every single one of the things he advised me to do gave me an incredible sense of self and inner strength and love. I have never seen the way he's able to love people repeated in any other being on this planet. It gave me this huge sense of, "Oh my God, I wish I could go out and through my music spread that love and service to humanity—even if it's only a hundredth of the depth of love he felt for me." He was an incredibly gifted person, a businessman, grandfather, yogi, a master of sound. He encompassed so many facets that people from all walks of life—every profession, every expertise you could think of—could be advised by him because he was truly a living master.

Even though he knew I was good at singing but maybe not so good at other things, he still infused me with the sense that I must serve in the highest way my being is capable of. He saw a person's potential and talked to that. So now here I am today with this sense that I can do anything, I can serve. I have this inner strength because of the faith and trust he had in me. He never gave up on me.

He was an incredible singer. He really knew how to sing from the heart, and sing *to* the heart. He also taught thousands of people to sing who thought they could never sing, through the practice of Kundalini Yoga. I teach chanting that same way, because it's about moving energy through your body.

If someone comes to your Nada Yoga workshop, what can they expect to learn?

Nada is the divine sound current. I would hope they would experience that inner resonance of truth. In these sacred chants we're vibrating sacred names of God, which is essentially helping people tune in to a higher frequency within themselves. We teach a Kundalini Yoga class to get the energy flowing, and then practice meditation and chanting. That raises the energy and brings healing to emotional body, the mental body, the physical body, and to the planet. Each Kundalini Yoga class is an actual prayer for peace on the planet itself, because sound is something that radiates out and never stops.

You're very active in the interfaith movement, bringing people from all religious traditions together to sing and pray.

Peace is something that requires people of all faiths to come together and understand each other. That became especially apparent after September 11th. People in the Sikh community wear turbans. In Eugene, my home town, they were being mistaken for Islamic fundamentalists. I also felt we had to protect our Muslim friends. So it was a very sad time and also a scary time. I became very active in reaching out to the interfaith community to create dialogue so that people could know who we were, that Sikhs stand for peace. Sikhs believe in peace through strength. Don't be afraid of anyone and don't make anyone afraid of you.

When people come to hear you sing they see a woman wearing a turban and no makeup. Some are intrigued, others are uneasy.

People often ask me, "Why do you wear that turban and those clothes?" I could answer, "I wear it because I'm a Sikh and this is our traditional dress," but there is something deeper. I wear them so I can remember to be a kind person. I learned that from Yogi Bhajan because he was all about remembering who you are. You don't just leave your spiritual practice in the meditation room and go out and act like a jerk. The idea of wearing this turban and this white cloth is to bring the energy of meditation with me consciously on a physical level. This is who I am and this is the spirit I carry.

It has an effect on other people too. For example, in high school I was never hit on by any guys. There was a certain level of respect. People wouldn't swear around me. Wearing this allows me to carry my practice into my daily life and allows other people to realize, "Oh, this is the way she's living her life."

What does your name mean?

My name was given to me by Yogi Bhajan. Snatam means "universal" and it means "one who has the strength and capacity to be a nucleus." It's one who's able to relate to all the different walks of life, all different ways of being, with love and respect, yet maintain a central identity of the self within all of that. Our spiritual names are given to us as hukams, as commands. That way when people call, "Hey Snatam, you need to do the laundry," I'm still being identified with that essential meaning that's my destiny. It calls me to live in that light.

You recorded a CD with your mother. I read that when you were a child you asked her, "Where is God?" and she answered, "Here in the music."

We're kindred spirits. When I grew up she played kirtan in the house all the time. It was part of waking up in the morning and going to sleep at night. Making that CD almost felt like singing with myself, a reflection of my own energies.

My mother taught me from a very young age if I ever needed comfort I should go to the sound current. I'd go to the family temple and sit there for hours and just sing until I felt better. That was a technique I learned from her, and I'm so grateful.

You were named a semi-finalist for a Grammy. What is it about your music that's appealing to such a broad audience?

People want a sense of inner peace. I find people who've never been to a yoga class before or done spiritual activities from the East, are still drawn to my music because it makes them feel relaxed. People come up to me and say, "I play it in my office all the time," or "When I put it in the CD player in the car, the kids stop screaming." If I'm wearing a turban and singing words they're unfamiliar with, they don't care as long as they feel that sense of joy inside.

Yes, but people can go and listen to classical music or light jazz and relax. Something different happens when you're performing. There's a whole other dimension there.

I've always tuned in to the presence of my guru when I sing, and I feel his whole energy. I feel there are angels surrounding me and everyone else there. I encourage people to tap into that divine presence that's with us all the time. When I was quite young I would imagine an angel chorus coming in and singing with me because I really, really felt the divine presence. When we tune in with our concerts, I pray for the presence of my guru to come, I pray for the presence of Jesus and whatever spirits are necessary for the upliftment of that particular crowd, to bring them to their hearts.

Kirtan really helps to open people's hearts right away. Sometimes I find the kirtan is the thing that's carrying us. At times I'll close my eyes and get so into the kirtan that I won't at that moment remember where we are, because that space is so infinite, and just about love. There's no time and space there.

The energy of chanting is energy moving upwards, so it's really important after you finish chanting to take a moment to be silent. Recognize the sacred space that's been created and ground yourself there. Use the chant to go beyond all boundaries, to break through to pure awareness.

Guru Nanak was born at a very violent time in Indian history, when northern India was under attack by foreign invaders. The Siri Guru Granth Sahib *is full of his songs calling for inner peace, the only force that can create lasting peace in the outer world. I love your music and I love your message, and I'm deeply impressed by how powerfully the Guru's words channel through you.*

I know the power of sound and prayer from my faith, and I know the power of sound from other people's faiths. I know this power to be very real.

Ragani

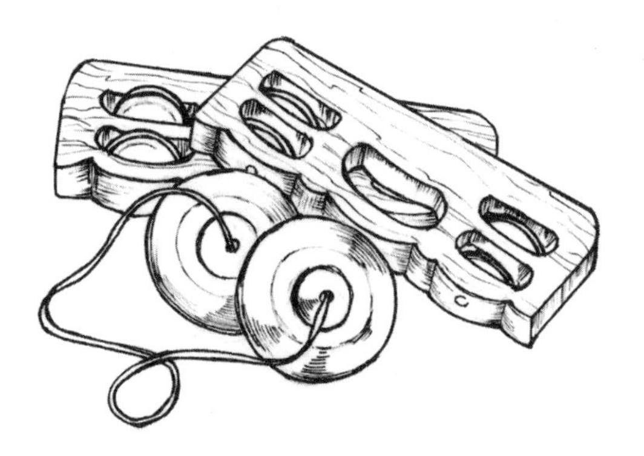

Ragani

Kirtan in California? Or at the classy, popular yoga centers in New York City? That doesn't necessarily surprise anyone; America's two coasts have always warmly received influences from the East: yoga, Sufi dancing, Ayurveda. But what about conservative middle America?

It turns out kirtan is booming in the Midwest. In fact, Milwaukee has the largest independent and ongoing kirtan community in the country. New kirtan groups are constantly springing up in big cities and little towns throughout the heartland.

A major force behind the surge of chanting in the Great Plains is Ragani, whose debut CD *Best of Both Worlds* was ranked 4th place, "Best Asian Ethnic Album" at the Just Plain Folks 2004 Music Awards, the biggest international music awards program in the world. It was singled out from over 10,000 albums worldwide.

Ragani is one of the most gifted and committed kirtan singers on the scene today—in fact, she's co-founder of the International Kirtan Foundation, which helps promote sacred chant around the planet. Her music has been featured on NBC and FOX television programs, and in a host of magazine and newspaper articles. A documentary film, *Fifteen Rainbows,* which highlights Ragani's kirtan, is scheduled for release in 2007.

Ragani's non-music related resume is impressive too: she has a Ph.D. in Clinical Psychology and runs a successful acupuncture practice in Milwaukee. Her husband, Dale Buegel, M.D., is a leading alternative health practitioner and author.

Often when yoga students attend Ragani's kirtans for the first time, they have the uncanny sense that she looks familiar. That's because Ragani is also famous as a Hatha Yoga model; her image, gracefully balanced in one hatha posture or another, has appeared in numerous magazines. She was also featured in the top selling *Yoga: Mastering the Basics* book and DVD.

Ragani was classically trained in Indian music, though she performs traditional call-and-response kirtan with a Western sensibility that makes it exceptionally appealing to the American ear. She first learned kirtan from her guru, Swami Rama of the Himalayas. Swami Rama, one of the most influential yogis of the 20th century, is best known for demonstrating his yogic abilities (such as perfect control over his brain waves, heart beat, and body temperature) under rigorous scientific scrutiny. But Swamiji (a respectful term for a swami) loved devotional music, and invited Ragani along with him on his world travels to sing and play the harmonium. He encouraged her to make sacred music her life mission at a time when hardly anyone in the Western hemisphere had heard of this form of spiritual practice. Today Ragani's biggest challenge is finding a venue large enough to accommodate all the enthusiasts who line up to join her hugely popular kirtans.

What drew you to this kind of music?

When I was in eighth grade I was babysitting for a woman who used to teach yoga classes. She had a kirtan in her home. The music sounded so hauntingly familiar. I was hooked from the moment I heard it.

How is it that kirtan can reach out and grab people like that?

People want to return to the sacred. The world needs more heart. Kirtan answers that need. It cuts across a lot of genres. The kirtan I do is not out of any particular religion, it's more the sound, the vibration, the tradition of it that touches people, so when they're exposed to it they feel it's for everyone. We may come from different religions or backgrounds, but we're all looking for that same connection to spirit, to the source. Kirtan is a way of reconnecting to yourself. People really need that.

I'm always impressed at how ecumenical kirtan is. The hall is filled with people from every faith, and people with no religion at all. They're all totally into the music.

One of the Lutherans who came to our kirtan and loved it, worried whether his minister would approve. Then he found out his minister had been coming longer than he had. They just hadn't seen each other there! We also had a conservative rabbi come to our kirtan on a Saturday. He talked about some very interesting parallels with the Jewish tradition and the use of sacred language and sound. Anyone can adapt kirtan to their own background and translate it into the spiritual context with which they're most comfortable.

How do you think chanting works? It seems to lead people to peaceful or even blissful states.

The kirtan that Swami Rama taught me was from Nada Yoga, the science of sound vibration. We repeat a sacred sound over and over until it creates a groove in the mind. It resets our physiology, the energy, the alignment of our body. When you generate this back and forth groove of call-and-response between the kirtan leader and the participants, it helps to realign the *nadis* (the currents of energy in our subtle body). Then when you rest in the silence after the singing, you can feel the energy of the vibrations.

With yoga science you create a pattern in the mind, and you can actually realign yourself mentally and spiritually. I've often compared it to jogging. You wouldn't take a three-minute jog. You need to go longer to get the body into a rhythm. It's the same when you want to bring the mind into a rhythm. Once you get that rhythm going you start feeling the effects of it.

You don't have to know what we're singing. Asking what the Sanskrit words mean is like saying, "What does Linda mean?" Even if people come and don't sing, they can still benefit because the sounds they're hearing will draw them into that groove. I suspect even if someone were deaf, their energy would still be affected.

When people first arrive at a kirtan, the energy is all over the place. People came from work or from school, some people are happy, some are sad. It's a whole room of people talking, just chatter and scattered energy. It feels almost a little edgy. Some people don't want to calm down. If they've never been to a kirtan before they're wondering, "Is this going to be boring?" They sit in the back to make sure they can escape if they decide to leave. I joke when we start, "Randy, lock the doors. We're going to chant the same thing over and over again for hours." You can see the newcomers feeling a little nervous.

But when we start chanting, it's like a wave. If you start swirling water in the same direction, suddenly all the water in the bowl is flowing together. If the baby is fussing and you rock it, it stops crying and relaxes. Like rocking a baby, this back and forth, call-and-response experience of kirtan soothes and rejuvenates the mind and heart. It has an organizing effect on the mind and body.

When you have a lot of people doing the same thing energetically, it creates a really powerful force. That's why both kirtan and meditation are even more powerful when you do them in a group. You get this whole force, this kind of ride that's bigger than all of us individually. It takes you right into the center, into that quiet space. It stills the mind.

When you go to a rock concert and there are 20,000 people there, everyone gets in a sort of mob consciousness that teeters on violence at times. In kirtan the group energy aligns but it takes you to a place that's deeply serene and even sublime.

There's something about kirtan, these mantras we use, that takes you to a different place. It's like electricity. You can use it to rev things up or to cool things down. The purpose of kirtan is to bring people to an elevated state of inspiration so they may feel more awakened, or they may describe it as being more peaceful or calm. But it's very different from that pounding, yelling, and shouting at some rock concerts, where you leave feeling exhausted. Often people say when they wake up the next morning, the kirtan songs are still going through their head. It's almost as if they're a little bit high for a few days.

In a rock concert you just want to pump up that energy and then leave your audience there. What do you do with the energy now? Well, you go do more drugs and have more sex, or do wheelies (car stunts) out in the parking lot. Not many people do wheelies after kirtan.

I'm in an altered state for a few days after a kirtan and I'm always curious why it fades. Swamiji used to tell me to watch how long that state lasts, how long you're able to hold it, because that tells you how many holes there are in your pot.

When you get that energy going back and forth between the musicians and the participants, it allows that energy of love to come in. Whatever we are starts to unfold. Then when you slow the music down and stop it, that's when people start to feel stuff, and that stuff is *you*! We're not doing anything except quieting the mind, and when we become still, that's *you* you're feeling, that energy inside you that feels bigger than your body, that feels like it goes through the roof. That's who all of us really are. People will say, "We feel so much love in this room." It's true.

I think of Swamiji a lot when I'm doing kirtan. That energy reminds me of being with him.

How did you meet Swami Rama? Was he the one who taught you how to do kirtan?

I met him when I was eight at EastWest bookstore in Chicago. My mother led the way with yoga and vegetarian cooking. She was on the cutting edge culturally. We were vegetarians before it was known that you could eat vegetarian food and still be healthy! My grandmother used to try to stick ham in my sandwiches because she thought I'd grow up weak!

Swamiji became a real presence in my life and I would spend my summers at his ashram in Pennsylvania. Sometimes I'd organize a little group that used to go up to the ashram chapel and do the kirtan. When Swamiji heard about that, he started giving me lessons in Indian music. In Western music they do very choppy notes, but in Indian music they'll curve around the notes of the scale. It brings tears to my eyes remembering those moments with him.

He started leading the kirtans himself, but he began teaching us new songs like "Hare Krishna Govinda." I didn't like those songs because nobody knew the words. The Sanskrit phrases were too long and difficult, so nobody sang. It frustrated me because it lost the group feeling. This went on for an entire summer. I just wanted the old, simple songs. I still to this day feel this way—that's why we keep all our songs short and simple. I want people to only have a few phrases so they don't have to think about the words, and can just release themselves to the mood. Westerners lose the feeling of the kirtan if they have to focus on a lot of foreign-sounding words.

That summer at one of the kirtans, Swamiji had been singing all these new chants and then he stopped. I opened my eyes and he was looking right at me. I felt his gaze go right through my heart. Then he started singing "Sita Ram," my favorite chant. He was singing with all this incredible love. It was the most personal, intimate connection—he was singing for me! It still chokes me up. I can still feel him looking at me.

That year he brought over a classical Indian music teacher, Tiwariji. Several times a day I would meet with him and he went through the ragas and took me through pretty intense training. I was doing three to six hours of practice a day then. Swamiji told me to go with Tiwariji to Curacao to continue my studies. I said "Swamiji, I love music but I didn't come here for music, I came here for you." He said, "Don't be foolish! Decide what you're going to do.

I'll give you till tomorrow. But you should go and study music. Opportunity only comes once, remember that." I went to Curacao.

In Curacao, I had several hours a day of music lessons and teaching yoga. Swamiji would call every morning and ask how the practice was going. He'd want to hear something and had me send him tapes, which he critiqued. I'd been there for six weeks—I was supposed to be there for a year—then his secretary called and said, "Come home! Swamiji wants you to go to India with him!" We went to India, Malaysia, Singapore, Bangkok, and we did lots of kirtan.

Did Swami Rama give you the name Ragani?

Before I went to India that first time, he gave me all kinds of goofy names like Rakshasi (mischievous spirit) and Badmash (rascal), which he called everybody when he was teasing them. But then I went to him and said, "I think I've changed. I feel like I'm picking up somewhere where I left off long ago in some other life, like I'm coming home." He said, "Yes, good," and he gave me the name Ragani. *Raga* means "to give color to" or "give mood to," especially in connection with music. You could loosely translate it as "melody" but it means much more than that; it has all the richness of the time, place, space, and energy of the music. Ragani is the female form of raga. It's now my legal name.

I find myself swaying during kirtan. Did Swamiji want you to sit absolutely still?

Oh no, he did move and sway. But standing up seemed to change it for him. He'd go hard and fast on some of the chants, and he'd be moving and rocking and keeping his hand going with a fist to keep the beat, so he definitely wants the movement there. But he didn't want people to get up and dance. I don't stop people from dancing if they want to, but if you remain seated, then the moment we stop playing you can go into the stillness.

It seems to me a natural progression to go right into the silence. For Westerners who aren't familiar with yoga, it gives them a taste of meditation. We started calling kirtan "the back door to the divine" because it's such an easy way to go inside. Meditation isn't easy for a lot of people (when they first begin this spiritual practice), so when they go to a kirtan and then stop singing, they find that calmness or peace or love between the songs. They get a taste of inner life.

There's something delightful about bringing this Eastern tradition to Western minds, giving the experience to someone who doesn't really know much about it. They experience it with a kind of innocence that allows them to savor the essence of what it is in a very natural way. It's a short cut that goes around the cultural packaging and drops them right off in the center, and there they are.

I love the music, but the most powerful moment is when the music stops.

You feel the whole room go silent, and you sit there and your eyes are closed and you realize there are several hundred people in the room. You open your eyes and look out on a sea of faces and there's not one person you recognize, yet you feel connected to every one. Then you start chanting again and the vibrations aren't just coming from the outside, they're coming from inside your throat and your lungs and your heart and your whole being. Then you realize you can't tell where your vibrations end and the next person's begin. Your space extends. Kirtan shatters boundaries, and brings people back to their heart center.

When well intentioned but less skilled musicians try to lead a kirtan, and you've got a new group of people who don't know what kirtan is, and the music stops, you'll see people looking at each other asking what's wrong, did the electricity go out? In the West we're not used to just sitting quietly. What you do at some of your kirtans now, when you turn out the lights for one song and it's totally dark, and there's nothing in the room but an ocean of vibration as all the souls in the room chant the mantras together in complete darkness, that's absolutely awesome.

One thing I do after everyone's gone is close my eyes and feel the silence in the room. It's so beautiful. Here we were creating all this incredible sound and music and joy, and then it stops, people get up and leave, and now the room is empty again. I don't know why it moves me so much. The music was here and now it's going out into the world.

The gift that keeps on giving! In a sense your music is another one of Swami Rama's gifts to the world.

I don't think you can separate the kirtan and the guru. When we were recording the first CD, I did a retreat at a house in the wilderness. For two weeks I was by myself, and went for a walk every morning down the drive as if I was walking with Swamiji, even though he's no longer physically alive. I would talk to him in my mind, ask him if it was the right time to start the project. I'd wanted a sign that I was doing the right thing at the right time. In my mind I heard him say, "What would you like to see?" and I said, "A snake," because I thought it would be funny to see a snake in Wisconsin in the cold and snow of winter. "Don't be subtle; be obvious," I said to him.

That afternoon I went upstairs to the kitchen. In the middle of the floor was this huge snake like you see in the zoo. I'd forgotten what I'd asked for that morning, and I was thinking, "Holy cow, what's a snake doing here?" To get to the kitchen it would have had to go through two closed doors, and there it was sitting with its tongue sticking out. I didn't know if it was poisonous but I thought it would be just my luck: I pick it up, it bites me, I die. Then I remembered my request that morning and got goose bumps. I looked at the snake and I thought, "Who are you?" It was the most awesome, unbelievable thing! I wound up getting a broom and sort of sweeping him across the floor to the porch.

So I told Swamiji that I would be in charge of the music on the CD, but he would have to be in charge of getting the feeling into it, instilling the inspiration into the musicians. I always left a chair for him whenever we recorded. Sometimes people brought flowers—the ones who knew who the chair was for.

My big desire when I was young was to know someone who was enlightened, to see them live on a day-to-day basis, to witness the reality of their yoga, to see that in action. When Swamiji picked me up and started working with me, that was the answer to the one thing I really wanted. The rest of life feels like icing on the cake.

You love your guru very much.

When I think back on the essence of what Swamiji was for me—it was about love. That incredible connection to give the teachings so closely—such as when he would answer the door before I even pushed the buzzer, already knowing I had come. And about how we used to entice him out of his room with music, about how he watched us day and night—our actions, our thoughts—with incredible love and attention. The experience of being witnessed even in the absence of his physical presence—that experience had a profound impact and even took a little getting used to! It was for me the essence of the relationship that I carry with me into the kirtan. When we are witnessed in this close manner, we start to watch ourselves then too, and it becomes an intimate connection with the guru within.

People often ask me if my time with Swamiji was like a dream. It feels more like I'm dreaming now. What we had with him felt more real than anything else in my life. He used to give so much to us, in so many ways, and the most powerful work was done from the inside. There were times that I would go to see him with something in my mind or heart that I had not spoken to anyone. And before I would have a chance to even say anything, he would already be asking me about it.

For me, Swamiji's bottom line was love. He often spoke of the "language of love," and said that it is the universal language that is understood by everyone. He used to tell us to "grease everything you do with love," and I remember watching him do that in his life. I watched him knead dough for *chapatis* (unleavened Indian bread) when we were in Singapore, and the dough almost came to life with his love! I remember bringing a tub of sudsy water to him one afternoon to wash his hands before coming to lunch—we were all working in the yard that day. As I approached him, holding that sudsy water before me, he reached into the bucket with such love, took all the fluffy bubbles and put them on my cheek! That was his way. Everything was done from the inside.

There were evenings we'd just sit and listen to music. He would play Vaiyasaki Das' kirtan tapes and comment what good kirtan it was, that good kirtan is hard to do. He had such a love and soft spot in his heart for music, and he used to say that the voice was the highest instrument of all.

Sometimes when I wanted to see him, I would go sit outside his apartment in the U.S., or in a room next door in India, and start to sing. He loved the sound of the music, the classical sounds of the ragas, and we knew that. So I would sing to coax him out so that we could be with him. We'd start to sing, and soon we would hear him in his sandaled feet coming "thump, thump, thump," softly down the stairs to join in and sing with us. Music was like that for him.

Most music is about love, and mostly about romantic love. Kirtan is about divine love. We sing out our love for the divine, and in the perfect silence afterward we feel enveloped in God's loving response. I can see why great yoga masters like Swami Rama encouraged their students to do kirtan. It's the easiest, and probably the single most enjoyable, form of spiritual practice ever developed. You've been very active in promoting this practice worldwide. Tell us about your kirtan foundation.

The International Kirtan Foundation was established in order to promote kirtan in the U.S. as well as internationally. I was getting email from people saying "Hey, I'm moving to Alabama," or "I'm living in Georgia, do you know of a kirtan group here?" There are kirtan events all over the country but you have to look hard to find some of them. I thought it be nice to have a website that would be a sort of "Kirtan Central." It's called Kirtan Connection for now (www.KirtanConnection.com).

We're creating this major database where the kirtan leaders can go and have their own webpage, no matter how small their group is. They can put up any of their information, list their events, upload sound clips, and post information about CDs. The website will offer the general public information about events in their area and access to the kirtan scenes around the world.

We'll also have chat rooms and cross-links and places where we'll invite some of the prominent kirtan wallahs (singers) to come in and be interviewed. The long-range vision is to have a center set up to hold 5000 people where we can bring in major chant artists, and have ongoing kirtan with different wallahs coming regularly, along with yoga and other related activities.

Hey, when you get this going, I'm moving to Milwaukee!

Jai Uttal

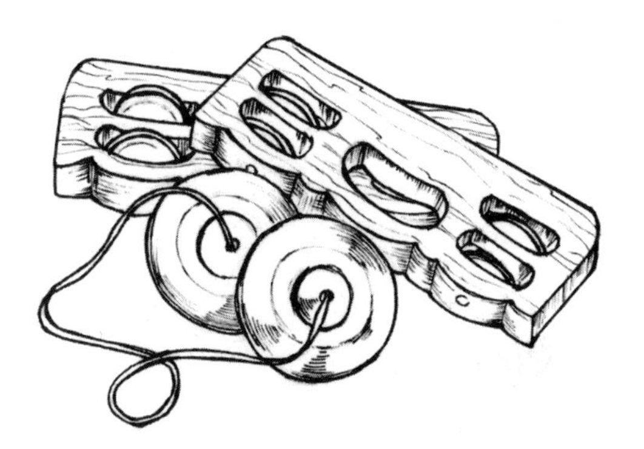

Jai Uttal

As I walk through Jai Uttal's Northern California home, I pass more than twenty instruments, half of which I've never heard of before. He introduces each one to me with a mixture of love, reverence and childlike enthusiasm, which is surpassed only by the joy he exudes when introducing me to his wife Nubia and baby boy Ezra.

I meet the one-stringed ektar and five-string fretless banjo, the droning tamboura and the wailing soprano twelve-string guitar, along with all the rest. Finally, I come to a little xylophone, which turns out to be baby Ezra's. Like Jai, the little boy is getting an early start on his exposure to music.

Jai began studying classical piano at the age of seven and later went on to learn old time banjo, harmonica, and guitar. He was a musical experimenter from the beginning, and has spent his life exploring a kaleidoscope of musical forms. At the age of eighteen he moved to California to become a student of India's "National Living Treasure," Ali Akbar Khan, from whom he received traditional voice training. You can detect this influence in Jai's trademark vocals which, the first time I heard them, sounded to me like the yearning of my own soul. With Khansahib he also studied the *sarod*, a complex, twenty-five-stringed Indian instrument with a haunting and mysterious sound.

At the age of twenty, Jai traveled to India for the first time and, as with many of his generation, the journey was transformational. While there, he met his guru, Neem Karoli Baba. He also steeped himself in the spiritually ecstatic music of the people. Both of these experiences have shaped his life ever since.

Like his extensive instrument collection, Jai's musical talent is vast, spanning everything from rock to the *Ramayana.* He recently undertook the massive visionary project of setting this ancient, epic Indian poem to music. He performed it with the Chicago Children's choir, for which he received critical acclaim from the mainstream media.

Jai is an internationally known kirtan leader and has produced dozens of CDs, both kirtan and of various other musical genres. His CD Mondo Rama, which contains Brazilian influences, Hebrew prayers, Appalachian Blues, Beatles psychedelia, along with Indian music and chants, was nominated for a Grammy as "Best New Age Album" of 2002. He has been a major contributing energy in the kirtan world, and is one of the foremost kirtan artists drawing a listening audience beyond the New Age or yoga crowd. In short, Jai's an impressive musical being.

And an amazing human being as well. Every time I talk with him, he emanates a mélange of humbleness, honesty, self-knowledge, passion—and sheer amazement at his life and the mystery of Life, qualities which are endearing. He is at once both transcendent and grounded. And he always seems to weave in a little laughter, which makes him eminently approachable.

I asked him what his name means. Uttal is Lithuanian and his birth surname. His Sanskrit name is Jai Gopal, which was given to him by a yoga teacher he had before he met his guru. "I guess that's why I'm not a 'Das,'" he jokes, referring to the fact that Krishna Das, Bhagavan Das and Ram Dass were, like him, devotees of guru Neem Karoli Baba (who devotees called "Maharaji").

Just as quick as he is to quip, however, Jai can turn reflective.

He tells me more about his instrument collection. "Emotionally, all the different kinds of instruments and music that I play and enjoy evoke different moods, different colors. I honestly feel that, since I was a teenager, all the music I was doing was directed—even if not totally consciously—toward inner healing, finding a place of wholeness. Each one has a different song, a different aura, a different world that emanates from it," he tells me in his soft voice that always seems to exude love and wonderment. "And they all inspire me in different ways. Some of them I've had for a really long time and some I haven't. But I look at them and they are like beings. I feel like on some level they are always singing and, you know, it's cool—whenever you sing in the house you can hear them resonating.

"I feel—this is kind of crazy, I guess—I really feel like instruments, particularly if they're played frequently, are sentient beings. Maybe it's because they're made from wood and other natural materials that they hold energy. Particularly old instruments; they just hold so much energy."

Jai was ahead of his time; he was into kirtan even before he hit India in 1971. His experience with the practice is extensive and even exotic. He's lived in India among the Bauls, the wandering street musicians of Bengal. He's led kirtan in countries as diverse as Israel and Fiji. He's sung with great singers and those with no musical ability whatsoever. He finds this broad spectrum of experiences the epitome of kirtan. "Sometimes kirtan is gorgeous and sometimes super rustic. It's all kirtan. The heart of what kirtan is is the prayer—the repetition of the mantra, of God's names, and the intention—being sung. But that singing can be two screechy notes or the most gorgeous classical raga (musical mood or melody). Whether it's sung, screamed or cried, it's all praise."

I'm intrigued by the time Jai spent with the mystical minstrels known as the Bauls. The origin of the name is debated, but one interpretation is that it comes from the Sanskrit word, *batul,* meaning "divinely inspired insanity."

Tell me more about meeting the Bauls and how they influenced you.

Before I ever went to India, amongst the albums of Indian classical music I had found was one called, "The Street Singers of Bengal." This record was so moving and transcendent. I also had one book called *The Bauls of Bengal.* It was a little history of them, and a collection of translations of songs. So between the book and this album, I had to meet the Bauls.

A friend and I went to Shantiniketan in West Bengal, which is a university town founded by Tagore (early twentieth century Bengali poet and Nobel laureate), who was a real proponent of the Bauls. The Bauls were society's rejects in Tagore's time because they were so outside of all the traditions. They were outrageous! Tagore said, though, "Hey, these guys are one of our national treasures." So the Bauls had begun to come more into popularity. In fact, two well-known Bauls are on the cover of Bob Dylan's *John Wesley Harding* album (1967).

So my mission was to find the Bauls. And I had no idea how. But I had heard they were living around this university town, so I went there. After several days of asking around and not getting anywhere, I was sitting in a *chai* (milky Indian tea) shop, drinking some tea. I saw this old man walking down the street, wearing a patchwork dhoti (strip of cloth wrapped around the loins and legs, tucked in at the waist to function like a loose pair of trousers). He was carrying a one-stringed instrument in one hand and a little drum that he was playing with his other hand, and had bells around his ankles. He came to the chai shop and played, and asked if anyone had any money. Afterwards, I followed him because this was the first Baul I had seen in person. And he was cool. And he was old, you know, and his singing wasn't beautiful, but he was radiant. Great energy.

We came to this place where there was this little *mela* (gathering). On stage there was this big family, and they were all sitting down except the lead singer, who was dancing. Each song had a different lead singer.

Sitting around on the floor were all the grandmas and grandpas, the little babies, all generations, playing cymbals and singing with him. And it was just great. And the guy gets off the stage and it turns out he's one of the guys from Bob Dylan's album! (Laksman Das Baul).

So I made his acquaintance and met the others who were singing. We really connected with this one guy, Baidyanath Das Baul. He started coming to our house and we arranged for him to come four times a week and give us lessons. Of course, we knew no Bengali and he knew no English but we began to have this amazing relationship over music, singing, chai, a little food, all kinds of instruments. He was teaching me so many different things—songs, rhythms, lyrics. Baidyanath would write them down, and later another friend who spoke English would translate them for us.

Word got out that there were a couple of Americans who loved the Bauls. We didn't have much money but we were always cooking food. And so daily we had itinerant groups of Bauls—well, they're all pretty much itinerant—coming to our house, singing and partying. Some of them were wonderful, and some were super-obnoxious, trying to get money from us. It was a real variety. But what a time it was! It was so rich and a beautiful time. I also became friends with other Bauls and spent time wandering around with them. They go from place to place, playing and asking for alms in exchange for their songs. So I did that with them. I had written some Baul-style songs, with Baul melodies and instruments, but with English words. And I would play some of them. It was just amazing.

Not only was it a super-profound human experience for me, meeting these people and getting very close to them and being with them, it was also really inspiring musically. Their music is simple but full of passion, full of energy. Their words are very metaphorical. A lot of the songs are very veiled in different kinds of imagery. A lot of tantric stuff. The imagery that's used is very rural, rustic. But their tone is a tone that's busting out, that's breaking through the rooftops of heaven.

Toward the end of our time there, we met Purna Das Baul, who was pretty famous in the West. He was the other Baul on Dylan's cover. Purna Das was opening what he called a Baul University. (Jai laughs.) You've got to imagine: two huts with roofs made out of straw. But it's where he wanted to teach Baul music. It had been a tradition passed strictly from guru to disciple. He had a little ceremony and he proclaimed that my American friend and I were "international Bauls." He gave us a little garland. It was so cool.

It was a big, important time in my life. Rhythmically and melodically, that music has really influenced me. I have some of my own versions of Baul songs. (He cites, among several other songs, "Malkouns" on his Beggars and Saints album and both "Corner" and "Bhajore" on Shiva Station as having Baul influences.) That was a lot of mileage I got out of my first immersion!

When you talk about the Baul scene you came upon, of everybody on the stage, it makes me think of the time I saw you and your band (The Pagan Love Orchestra) playing in that club in Berkeley. There were lots of musicians on the stage and you were standing and playing the harmonium. And it was so joyful! And fun!

The Pagans were definitely in part fashioned after a Baul band. No one else in the group has that familiarity with the Bauls, but in my mind, in my concept, that's a lot of how I wanted them to be—musically loose and a festive, communal gathering. That was the vision. Of course, with electric instruments!

It seems that most everybody who went to India in that time period was going as a spiritual seeker. It sounds to me like you were going there as much a musical seeker. You had so much background in Indian music before you even went.

For me, there's never been a distinction—literally, the spiritual seeking has always been absolutely hand-in-hand with the music. I was searching for the Bauls because their music awakened so much spirituality and connection. So searching for them was no different than spiritual seeking. In the way that someone might seek out a *lama* (Tibetan guru) for teachings, I was seeking out the Bauls for teaching. Even with Maharaji. He didn't sing, but the kirtan was so much a part of the experience with him.

All I can say is that they weren't different pursuits. They've never been, even when I was younger and got into the banjo. I didn't have any concept of spiritual stuff then, but it soothed my soul and woke up my soul. They weren't ever two different journeys. They've always been the same journey.

What do you feel is the essence of the kirtan experience? What's happening for you during a live kirtan performance?

You could ask me every year and I'd have different answers. It's always evolving. How I feel these days: the heart of the practice is surrender. Surrender of my ego, my self, my will, my controlling nature, my own agenda, my heart. Surrendering it all at the feet of the infinite, my guru, God. Saying it over and over again, "Thy will be done. Thy will be done. Thy will be done."

Sometimes I'll be singing and it will be so high. Other times it's a struggle to relax in my voice and my body. But regardless of what I'm experiencing, in my mind I'm constantly offering.

What do you hope to convey to people through kirtan?

On the deepest level, I'm not trying to communicate with people. With my heart and soul, I'm trying to communicate with God. On another level, I'm opening my internal doors and inviting everybody to join me. Everybody is establishing their own communication with God. The practice of kirtan allows that. I'm not telling you to do this and you'll be happy. If anything of substance gets communicated to people who come to kirtan, that substance comes from the depth of that internal practice. If I'm singing to the group, they just get me, my ego. If I'm singing to my guru, then people get that. And they're singing to their own guru.

When we sing mantras we're joining the energy, adding to the energy, and also are fed by the energy of the ages. When we sing "*Om Nama Shivaya*"–one of the ancient mantras–we're adding our hearts and our energy to this ancient prayer for peace. Our voices are going out into the universe, and at the same time our hearts are being nourished by the energy of people who have sung this before. You can't really hold this idea in your mind, but it feels really true to me.

There seems to be a certain magic that happens when we sing in a group.

Kirtan has been practiced in groups for millennia. When the group all feels like one voice, you feel the divine presence. It's shining in all the molecules. It is super-high and beautiful. But that feeling of high is different from the high of drugs and alcohol. It's so much a feeling of the divine presence. I always feel like we're giving so much of our hearts to each other, our spirits and our passion. Most of us live life on a pretty low burner. When we can share that heart energy, the flame rises and it's just so great. If you're singing with an open heart, the presence of God, the divine spirit, the universal spirit—whatever you want to call it—is in the chants. The more we invest our hearts in the chants, the more that spirit is there. When you do it in a group, each person increases the others' experience.

Kirtan is an extremely healing thing, from my own experience. I had been singing kirtan before I met my guru, but when I met him the practice was empowered inside of me. But I still have had lots of karma to work out. I've had some dark periods in my life. But the practice of kirtan has kept me connected to God, to my guru, and kept me alive. And I can only express gratitude to my guru, and all those ancients. I'm not doing anything new—maybe adding a new drumbeat. But the essence of what I'm doing is the same as it's been for thousands of years.

You mentioned dark periods and that kirtan was your lifeline.

I met Maharaji when I was twenty. I can't imagine a greater emanation of unconditional love. In some ways, my life started at that point. My spiritual life. On an emotional level, I was raised with such a strong feeling of self-loathing and worthlessness and shame. So it took a really long time for me to know that Maharaji's love was coming through me as well. I always knew that it was there and that after I died I was going to go to Maharaji's blanket. But I felt that this time around I wasn't meant to be happy. I wasn't meant to feel love and joy.

As a kid, I thought enlightenment was becoming a different person. It was en-like-ment. I thought this whole spiritual thing was going to recreate me into someone I'd like more. (Jai halts, contemplating how open to be, then launches forward, sharing that he was in a bad marriage for seventeen years and at that time got heavily involved with drugs and alcohol.) And all the while, I was doing what I do (kirtan). But I know it kept me alive.

Kirtan is the way. It was the way for me to grab hold of something, of the spirit of my guru. Before I had no way to reach out. Now it was like I was reaching out for salvation, tangibly grabbing hold of Maharaji's foot through the song, through the voice, through the kirtan. Like throwing out a rope, in a way. And I didn't know of any other way to throw out the rope.

My under-psyche said I wasn't worth the grace I had been given, and I was trying to prove that to be true. And then my marriage fell apart. I went to a drug treatment program, which was very, very difficult.

That was in 2001 when I was forty-nine. It meant re-starting my life in so many different ways. But in that process I finally got so deeply in touch with all those underlying feelings that had been motivating my life for so long. I was beginning to see them clearly because *I* was getting clear. I went into this place of, "I'm falling! Catch me!" And I was caught. And I started living my life in a new way. And I felt very, very vulnerable, very young, and very dependent on God. And then I started feeling hope. I started to see that joyousness and love were there inside me. The only effort it took was to stop burying it.

That was when I met my wife, Nubia. I felt, "Wow, I can love and I can be loved. And I can trust that." Even now, at times when I wake up feeling kind of funky, I think of my life—and feel gratitude.

I think many people can relate to what you've just shared.

The more I talk about this stuff, the more I find there are people who really are grappling with the same thing. But they never have anybody to talk to about addiction in the yoga world, because people in the yoga world just don't talk about it. But at the end of almost every kirtan retreat I lead, there's someone who comes up who wants some guidance specifically about addiction. So I feel it's a great thing to be able to share all this with people. Talking about it heals it.

Kirtan also heals a fear of singing, or the feeling of not being a "good" singer. I know you address this topic too at your "Kirtan Camp" workshops, where you teach people to lead kirtan.

I'll often ask a group, "How many of you are afraid of your own voice?" Almost everyone raises their hand. In Western culture we're intimidated by emotions, and by expressing our emotions in song. Forget it! It's not like that in other cultures; it's not like that in India. But people in the West are getting over it. The first thing is to admit the fear. When you do, you can just sing. It's liberating. It's beautiful. The practice of opening one's voice and letting the feelings out is so great.

Most of us don't sing in our daily life. There's something liberating about singing—not just kirtan, but singing. Singing from the heart, expressing your feelings, breathing deeply. There's a rush that is very joyous. Maybe it's like God flirting. You get that rush and it is great.I really viscerally experience the power of the ancient mantras.

But even the mantras without heart, so what? Kirtan without bhakti, that calling of the heart, doesn't really mean anything. But of course the practice of kirtan can transform your heart. Any kind of singing that comes from that deep place is bhakti. It's the yearning to connect deeper, deeper, deeper with the spirit. That can sometimes be a real feeling of love, can be a real feeling of sadness, of anger, can be any feeling, but wanting to free it, free it, free it, letting the feelings of the heart burst open and be free and whatever they are, be like birds that take us closer to the spirit. Maharaji never gave lectures, but he gave clues. We would ask Maharaji, "What's the best form to worship God?" and he said, "The best form to worship God is every form. The only important thing is how much you love God."

Kirtan is so multi-level in the way it works. There's the whole psychological, cathartic aspect of getting in touch with one's feelings, and then putting them into song and using the voice to free them. You don't need any sense of God or a spiritual path. For most of us, that's a big head trip anyways. The spirit is so beyond the human mind. Most of our thoughts of it are colored by the limitations of the mind.

Singing is emotionally liberating. People who have never sung before come for the first time and they start crying in ten minutes. It's the opening. It's beautiful and wondrous. You don't have to ascribe to Krishna or Rama. It's just a release in your own heart. That's the core of what I think is spiritual anyway: the heart.

I've been doing mantras for thirty-five years. Mantra can be our life raft across a sea of turbulent despair. I don't know where mantras came from, but they weren't just made up by some fool on the street! I believe they were divinely channeled. And in the ancient days I believe the yogis and the sages were way, way, way in tune to the divine energy. The stuff that came through them was life saving tools, heart saving tools, soul saving tools.

You spent time with a modern-day sage, Maharaji (Neem Karoli Baba).

There was something about breathing that atmosphere, the atmosphere of being in the presence of such a holy man. It's a doorway to infinity. It changes all your molecules. But there was background music to it. Constantly kirtan. It's always pulling you deeper into your heart. The heart behind the heart. That I think is where kirtan takes us. We use our emotional heart. It's what fuels us. And then we go to the heart behind that, which is the eternal ocean.

Dave Stringer

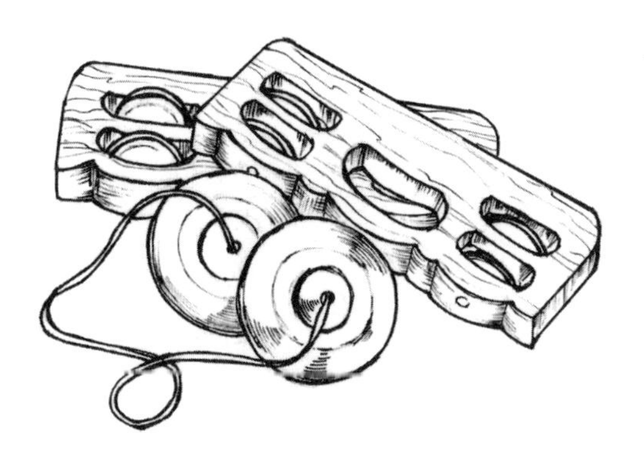

Dave Stringer

"Once you see it, you can't unsee it." Dave Stringer quotes those words from author Arundhati Roy to sum up the moment his life changed in an Indian ashram in 1990. Pre-India, Dave was a film editor living in Los Angeles. Post-India, he is a passionate kirtan wallah and world-traveling troubadour, singing Sanskrit love songs of and to the Divine.

He arrived in India not as a seeker, but as a hired hand. He went to the Siddha Yoga ashram in Ganeshpuri not for devotion, but to work on an editing project. In the process, he encountered kirtan for the first time. In kirtan "you're not just listening to the music, you *are* the music," he told me. The experience was so powerful he left his former life behind. "While I was at the ashram, my priorities began to change. I lost my reasons to do what I was doing in L.A."

"I was hired to go to India as a film editor. This was a job. I went there and encountered kirtan, and had a number of experiences that were sufficiently ecstatic and transformational that all those things I had going on in my life ceased to be important any more. This was the most riveting thing that I'd ever encountered.

The fact that I encountered it without seeking it and without believing in it and it still affected me and changed my life is significant.

"In a scientific culture, we examine things; we don't take things on faith. My approach to yoga has not been to take it on faith. But every time I chant I always feel better. And my experience keeps validating this."

After several months in India, Dave returned to L.A., but not to business as usual. Instead, he embarked on the spiritual path of kirtan, which became his career. His goal is nothing short of bringing this ecstatic, soulful experience to everyone on the globe.

To this end, Dave tours the world incessantly, singing kirtan in small towns and large cities, in yoga centers and smoky rural bars. It's all part of his philosophy that the sacred is in everyone, in every place. Therefore, he believes his role is to make kirtan as accessible as possible, both literally—by traveling a full third of the year to as many locations as humanly feasible, and artistically—by expanding the presentation of the practice beyond the form as we know it in the West. In that sense, he is a kirtan maverick, constantly pushing the envelope with the goal of inviting an ever-widening audience to experience the divine vibration. This audience includes even prison inmates, whom he has taught meditation and chanting.

Time, Billboard, In Style, and *Yoga Journal* have all recognized Dave Stringer as a top player in American kirtan. He has collaborated with numerous other artists including Rasa, Donna DeLory, Toni Childs and Girish, and has performed with Krishna Das and Jai Uttal. You can also hear his voice on the soundtracks of the blockbuster movie Matrix Revolutions and the video game Myst.

You spend a lot of time on the road.

Swami Muktananda (a guru in the Siddha Yoga tradition, where Dave first encountered kirtan) walked the length and breadth of India looking for his guru. Along the way he met lots of sages and saints. Each one taught him something. After years of this, he finally found his way to the home of the person who did initiate him, where he realized the truth of his own being.

That's a very Indian way of getting at it. I am a Westerner and I live in America. Here we have an inter-state highway system, a very sophisticated network of airports, Internet, cell phones. And I'm not looking for a guru. But it has been an article of both faith and experience for me that every person I speak to can point me toward the truth. And so, what I'm seeking doesn't exist out there, but exists in here. It's within myself. And I'm encountering all these people as an extension of myself.

I try to look at each one in their own way as saints and sadhus (holy men). Most of them are not pretending to be a holy person. But in meeting all of these people, I keep seeing the One, again and again. And it enlarges my sense of how we're connected and my awareness of myself, my compassion for other people, my sense of joy and ecstasy in connecting with other people.

I'm seeking an experience of my own inner Self that in effect is available anywhere. And each one is pointing me in a direction that I'm already going. We're at the very beginning of something new, which is the experience of communities of like-minded people coming together to sing with an awareness that's beyond a particular spiritual path.

If kirtan is going to continue to be framed in terms of guru and disciple, or even in terms of yoga, there are people who are not going to come. And those are often people who actually don't know they want this experience, but they do. They just don't recognize it when it's framed as yoga or devotion. I'm finding that by freeing it, by looking at kirtan from the perspective of art and the perspective of science, I'm able to penetrate more deeply into American culture. It casts another light on it.

Part of what this touring has been about is a community-building exercise. The more I'm out there traveling, the more the millions of cross-connections occur. I see people again and again in different cities. It's like I'm creating—to use a brain metaphor—a bunch of neural hook-ups. My presence and the presence of other kirtan singers traveling around the country is creating community. I'm thrilled to be able to be present in all these places almost simultaneously. I've enlarged my sense of neighborhood to all of North America and parts of Europe and coming this fall (2006), Asia. I'm going to Tokyo, Kyoto, Shanghai, Hong Kong, Singapore, and Sydney.

You studied jazz music very seriously, as well as visual art. How do they affect your approach to kirtan?

What I've started to do now, artistically, is move my kirtans out of yoga studios to art spaces. My own experiences with kirtan began with encountering it as a musical form. I was attracted to it because of something I felt when participating in it. I'm trying to make it available as widely as possible, because it has been my experience that when you participate in a kirtan, something happens to you way beyond what you might have thought or believed. There's something really intoxicating and entrancing. I just need to get people in the door for them to have that experience.

If I stage a kirtan at the local art museum, it takes on an entirely different feeling. The questions people ask and the perspective from which people look at it are quite different. People are used to experiencing the spiritual through art. That's something art has mediated for a long time. At the same time, modern art in general is pointing us toward the shock of the new. I'm able to invite people to come and experience this as music and as a participatory work of art. The spiritual experience follows from that. We don't have to put the frame of spirituality around it.

Once I was invited by a yoga studio in Jackson, Mississippi—I was surprised there was a yoga studio there—to come and chant. When I got there, I was astonished to discover the kirtan had been booked not in a yoga studio, but in a bar. I was a little shocked, but trying to maintain my sense of decorum, I said, "Well that's a really interesting choice! Can you tell me what made you choose this place?" And she said, "Well down here most people don't know about chanting mantras. We figured they wouldn't go to a yoga studio. But you know they're used to going to a bar for music, so we thought we'd have it in the bar." And you know, her logic was right on. Take it to the people!

I frankly never thought I'd be chanting in a bar. And so I had to change my sensibilities right away and go, "Dave, is there anyplace where the Divine is not?" We chanted mantras with people drinking beer and smoking cigarettes. And you know, we had a great time. The place to look for the Divine is in the people coming together and singing together. And that happened at a bar in Mississippi.

Ashrams are nice, but it's a rarified environment where you get to retreat from the world and be spiritual without the distractions of the world. The hard work is to go and live your life. Drop your kids off at soccer practice, go to the grocery store, do your job, return your phone calls, deal with your mother-in-law—and see the energy of the divine.

Here's the thing: people have all kinds of ideas about what constitutes a sacred place. To me it has absolutely everything to do with your intention. The way I read the yoga scriptures is that there is no place that the energy of the divine is not present. No place. Your very intention to make a place sacred makes it sacred. It doesn't matter whether those people are stoned or not, whether they're checking kirtan out as art, whether they believe in it or not. What's sacred isn't dependent on whether people want to approach it as sacred or not. The energy of the Divine is still there.

Your attitude is pretty unconventional. Ironically, the very act of being unconventional follows the conventions of the bhakti (devotional) movement.

In India spiritual activity, including the songs to the Divine, was originally exclusive to kings and other higher classes. But the bhakti movement in the fifteenth century challenged that mindset, believing that all are equal and each individual could speak to the Divine. Common people were taught simple songs, the aim of which was to achieve a state of ecstatic union within oneself and within the company of fellow seekers. In part because it upended the caste system, this movement caught fire. Some of the world's first "rock stars" developed, ecstatic singers who could move a crowd. It turned into a genuine mass movement.

As long as you challenge traditional mindsets, you're staying true to the bhakti roots. But I know you're also interested in the intersection of science and spirituality.

One of the things that interests me about kirtan is this phenomenology of what happens to our state of consciousness, what happens in our brains. When we do kirtan, if you participate fully in it, even without knowing anything about it, you end up not only with a feeling of ecstasy but also a feeling of stillness when it's over. These changes occur in the activity in people's brains. Science has been able to look at that and say, "Wow. This isn't something that people are imagining. This is real." You can see their consciousness is in fact shifting.

I want to take the sum from the output from everybody's head and get an average waveform. Then I can project that onto a screen and as the collective consciousness changes, we can witness a real-time analog version. It becomes an act of mass biofeedback. You can visually establish the initial state of consciousness of the crowd, and watch it change over time.

Would that be different if the crowd was watching? What is the impact of people observing themselves? Kirtan is an interactive thing. It may be that watching what our brains do may actually deepen the effect.

It's been my experience that there are profound changes. When you come to chant, you're an artist, too. I want everybody in the room to fully be a co-creator of that art. This extends even to watching our state of consciousness. Where this all goes is a matter of experimentation and experience.

You're an intellectual, constantly crossing back and forth between the mystical and the scientific.

I guess there is a part of me that seeks to validate this in terms of other areas of inquiry, partly because I think it makes it more accessible to larger numbers of people. By looking at this from the standpoint of science—and there is a lot science in this—I think I reach an audience that would never get near the guru and yoga thing. I bring more people into this conversation and this experience.

How did you develop this experimental outlook?

I was about seven-years-old when it first occurred to me that I was a musician. When I was nine I had a reel-to-reel tape recorder. I recorded a copy of the Beatle's "Within You Without You," and then cut up the tape and put it back together in a different order. The technical term for this is musique concrète, but I was just a nine-year-old kid playing around. I've always been attracted to music with a transcendental quality, and felt that at some level I had to interact with it. Hence my cutting it up and putting it back together."

Given your penchant for upending the traditional order of things, I notice you like to break the rules, such as the one which says no harmonies are allowed in Indian music.

I would hear a harmony and sing it, so I was constantly getting in trouble for it at the Ganeshpuri ashram. They'd say it was my ego, but in a lot of ways it was my bliss. Somehow I needed to encounter this Eastern discipline and still retain my own essential nature with it. I had to be able to come at it from a place that made sense in light of my own journey and experiences. The experiences I brought to it were singing in a choir and playing the acoustic guitar around the campfire. To me, things like harmony are cues to Westerners to sing along.

What was great about the ashram in India was that they taught me to surrender to the music itself. And to give up this idea that it was about my individual expression and instead view music as an expression of something deeper, beyond the individual. But as a Westerner I had instincts related to sacred tradition that I couldn't get rid of. So eventually they showed me the door. They kicked me out! But when God closes a window, he opens a door. And suddenly there was a yoga studio in Santa Monica inviting me to do kirtan.

It seems you need to hold true to your Western roots, your scientific perspective, your vision of kirtan as an art form, and your unique approach to your own music because that's who you are.

It's about "What ground can one authentically hold?" I'm not a *brahmana* (upper caste Hindu), I'm not a priest, I'm not a swami. And I'm not a very good devotee either.

I have been practicing yoga for a long time now, and am certainly formed by the ideas of Eastern philosophy. But what I can most authentically be is an artist. And I would say, as an artist, I am exploring my spiritual awareness and experiences. I'm standing on different ground. I'm trying to make excellent, quality music with an audience of amateurs. I don't see that as being paradoxical. The idea here is that everybody is musical. That singing and music are something so fundamental to being human that, without it, we can scarcely be said to be human.

What if life was all a musical and you had to sing everything you said? What would that be like? Singing is deeper than language. Singing is deeper than conscious thought. It opens a doorway to something really fundamental in our feeling and spiritual being. And even if you're not a musician, the fact is you resonate with it. Everybody feels music. It means something to us, even if we can't say what it means. It's an imprecise language that somehow speaks very clearly.

My gig is to give people a direct experience of what it's like to be a musician. I just get you to sing and then you know what it's like. By enlisting a crowd of people as the "choir," together with a group of professional musicians, gives the participants a sense of being a musician.

There's something magical about the musical looseness of a live kirtan.

Nobody is conducting it. It's just happening. And, you know, somebody out in the audience can change that. If somebody out there starts clapping at a certain point, the kirtan can explode in a whole different direction. To sit before that intelligence really fascinates me, to see how that works, to make the kind of music that is not based upon a plan, but in a sense finds the statue in the stone. It finds the music that's already in the people who have come.

You know how sympathetic resonance works, right? You strike the tuning fork and the string tuned to that same frequency vibrates. So, we all have this artist self, this musician self, this awakened self, and you're already tuned to that. All it needs is somebody to come along and strike the "tuning fork" and it's like, "Oh! It's not over there, it's in here." What happens, happens inside of you.

I've heard about people who have had big shifts as a result of kirtan. You know everything can change in an instant. In a sense the kirtan is about that instant.

You know from personal experience how much people can change. You've told me before that you used to suffer severe depression.

Once I started chanting and practicing yoga *asanas* (postures) every day, it went away. Yoga and chanting were working with what was in my own head. It moderated my chemistry. I don't want to say it's cured me, but all I can say is I don't have bouts of depression anymore. Maybe I've created a different chemistry in my brain.

In the act of singing I can observe my thoughts. In singing I can detach. Detachment in itself is ecstatic. I mean, kirtan is a kind of mass catharsis. It's better than psychoanalysis in this way.

When we are singing together in kirtan, frequently people have the experience that time slows or alters in some way, or stops completely. This is an art form that in some ways can help us find a new kind of experience, give us a new kind of insight into the way the world is. Similarly when you're lost in song, voices are blending and you're fully in the experience, one can have a sense that even one's own body is illusory, that one is not in a place of separation. Whether one is having this experience or not, kirtan points you toward this awareness. So both the form and the experience of kirtan are pointing us toward understanding time and space in a new way.

In some ways, I'm trying to challenge the spiritual with the model of science. In the other direction, I hope to challenge the scientific world with some of the understandings of modern spirituality. So I guess with all the language of science and art and everything that I've been talking about, this thing of going out to meet all these people and travel is in and of itself a spiritual practice. What I've been doing—touring and performing and scheduling and booking and promoting—is actually a huge of act of yoga for myself.

By that I mean being focused on the place that I'm going, and at the same time, removing all attachment to it coming out in a particular way. It means taming the inner demons of my own desires and attachments and moods, and really being compelled again and again to find a tranquil place within myself. To hold a place of inner stillness and compassion within myself even amongst a whirl of activity.

I'm trying to find opportunity in loss, or to see how everything turns out perfectly. There's a lesson in everything. What I'm trying to get out of this is the discrimination to know when to surrender and when to stand firm, when I should take action and when I should refrain from action. So the very doing of this thing has in many ways helped me to embody the very experience that was so attractive about kirtan in the first place: this expansive sense of peace, the incredibly exciting and ecstatic sense of stillness. It's such a paradox.

I once asked you why you don't have a Sanskrit name like many other kirtan wallahs. You admitted you wanted a new name, but were told you already had a Sanskrit name: Dave. It's pronounced almost exactly like deva *(pronounced "Dave-uh") which means, among other things, "shining being." You really do shine when you sing.*

Kirtan is an inner reset button for me. Why I do this is that it makes me quiet. There's so much noise in my head most of the time, and when I sing it shuts off. I sit in a place of expansive silence that doesn't want to add anything, doesn't want to take anything away. It's happy just to be. It's both really exciting and really the opposite of exciting at the same time. It's this elevator going up and down at the same time. In that moment I feel weightless. I feel free of anxiety.

I used to have a private practice and now I practice in front of an audience. But almost always I'm able to deliver myself to that place night after night. And it's that which I'm cultivating. It's a place of ease and repose. It's a space that allows what's going to go. It's not defined by concept or expectation. And my feeling is that, if there is "enlightenment," it's somewhere in that space. And it may be holding that space all the time, even as the chaos in the world goes on around me.

I'm more able to be in that space, even in situations that don't involve singing at all. In this way is it a practice? Yes. It's a profound practice for how I live in the world. But sometimes it's just really fun. And that's cool, too.

Wah!

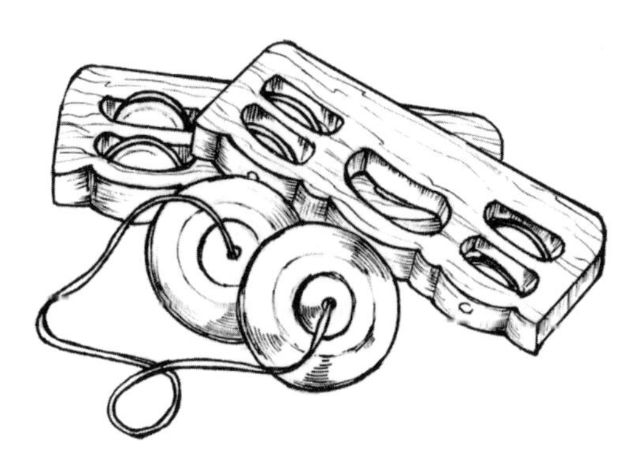

Wah!

When Wah! was a little girl she used to fall asleep on the floor of her family home while listening to her mother, a professional violinist, create music with her string quartet. "That was my feeling of love," she recalls. "I think the mother gives you your inner connection. And for me that was music."

For more than thirty years Wah! has connected through music—to herself, to her Self, to others, to the Divine—as a kirtan wallah. "I need to sing, I need the music, I need to feel the drums," she says. "Kirtan gives me the opportunity to connect with people and other healers. I do my healing with music."

Wah! is known for her diverse kirtan style that matches up all manner of musical genres with the traditional Sanskrit mantras, often in a playful manner, especially during a live experience. "For me, kirtan is different than japa (reciting a mantra). Kirtan is play among other beings, whereas japa is alone, personal," she told me. She attributes the roots of her playful approach to her father, a college professor who she says was also light-hearted and a lover of nature.

The passion for music sparked in her childhood led Wah! to the prestigious Oberlin College and Conservatory in Ohio where she majored in performance arts and minored in voice. After college, she was drawn to travel, live in an ashram, and study Eastern spiritual practices, all the while incorporating music into her experiences. A few decades later, she is an internationally-known kirtan leader and recording artist, having produced numerous CDs. Her 2002 CD *Opium*, was produced by Herb Graham, Jr., and supported by Macy Gray musicians and Alanis Morrisette band members. She travels the globe sharing her practice with a welcoming heart, and exuding the aura of someone in a place of mature practice and reflection that comes from real life experience. Wah's lavishly illustrated book, *Dedicating Your Life to Spirit*, offers her insights about yoga, self-exploration, and chanting.

Wah! presents a stunning, ethereal physical presence—serene, chiseled visage, liquid gray-blue eyes, tumbling spun-gold waves of hair, soft-spoken, petit, fine-boned—which is juxtaposed by intense character. Playful though she can be, there is a strong undercurrent of seriousness and discipline, which can come across as stand-offish. When she tells me she was rigidly strict in the early days of her spiritual practice, I have no doubt about the truth of that. And yet, as one talks with her, a softness and an open accepting comes through in her words.

Wah!'s celestial beauty and intense character meld with the wisdom that comes from thirty years of exploring life walking along a spiritual path. She shares this in a mellow, intimate way, whether it's one-on-one or with a hundred people during a live kirtan. Her style is philosophical; she talks lucidly about her explorations of the universal questions all seekers ask. She doesn't pretend to have the answers. Rather, she openly shares that she herself is a work in progress, which is extremely comforting to the rest of us far-from-finished masterpieces.

I'd like to share with you excerpts of my interviews with Wah!, including one that was done just after she had spent ten intensive days with her spiritual teacher, Amma (the "hugging saint" from South India), which left her in a particularly blissed out state.

My intention is to give you the opportunity to experience a slice of her essence, a bit of her Wah!-ness.

I have to ask this because everyone wonders. What does the name Wah! mean?

It means "bliss." It's about that expression of joy, that moment of perfection when you are completely connected.

It's such a unique name. How would you describe your kirtan music? What's unique about that?

It's female; that's the distinguishing characteristic. I've traveled with the guys a lot. Their kirtan tends to be linear and methodical. You know what you're going to get—it's sequential. The male energy is more linear and the female is more round.

Partly because I'm female and partly because of my personality, my kirtan is unpredictable. I rely a lot on the interaction with the audience. I'm not just presenting something; I'm trying to get inside their heads to see how I can uplift them or enhance their experience. I will improvise and play with the audience. I don't know if my erratic, playful nature is a result of being female, or if it's just a result of the soul.

Does being a mother impact your kirtan?

Does being a father? All the aspects of our lives, all our responsibilities have to be honored and be joy-infused. Being able to honor your responsibilities while still being of service to humanity is important; they're all connected. It's important to make sure that all the relationships in your life are clear, that you're working on them.

A lot of my playfulness has been shared with my daughter. We dance together and share stories. But she's becoming a teenager and now that playfulness, that loving kindness that I might have directed towards her, is directed out towards other people. To be able to manifest it with one person—a family member, or your lover, or whatever—is beautiful, and then to expand it out is a natural outcome of the practice. You go from personal love to universal love. You find it in one; then you find it everywhere.

You know, Mother (Amma) has a lot of playful energy, too, and has been able to feed and support that in me. (Wah! recounts a time when a tabla player sat in with Amma's band who, in Wah!'s opinion, was only there to show off his skill.) I'm like, "This guy's ruining this song!" And then I looked at the swamis and they were all smiling and laughing. They couldn't conceal their delight in seeing somebody try so hard to just be their best. It wasn't as judgmental as it was playful. That gave me a model to see how to bring my energy forward in a way that's full and yet not damaging to anybody. It's self-discovery.

You incorporate a lot of different musical styles into your kirtan, like reggae and jazz.

As a woman, I have lots of moods, and you can hear that in my music. If the energy stays the same for too long, it feels dead. If I play it the same way five times, I'm bored. I crave variety; I crave change.

The mantras are effective no matter what the music is. The music is different for different people's tastes. I offer different flavors so everyone can get it. Music is an expression of the soul, you know? Who you pick as a spiritual teacher says something about who you are and what you're working on. Who you like to listen to is the same.

Most kirtan singers play the harmonium when they lead kirtan, but you play the bass guitar.

I used to play the harmonium, but I got a repetitive injury in my wrist, and switched to bass. Who I am is very etheric. I really enjoy the quality of the bass; it grounds who I am and gives me the ability to manipulate the lowest and highest frequencies of the music.

You spent time in Africa a few decades ago. Where does that fit in?

Totally in the drumming. I'm playing the bass for a reason. I want to connect right in with that drummer. For a long time—and sometimes even now—we use the *ejembe*, because it's connected with African rhythms.

I feel very close to Africa. In Africa, the tradition is to wake up and drum. Through drumming and dance elders go into higher states. Kirtan is not different than that. The process is the same.

How would you describe kirtan to someone who's never heard of it?

It's an Indian hootenanny. It's a sing-along. For yoga practitioners it's a fun meditation practice you do as a group. The emphasis is on fun. It's not serious, but you do have a meditative experience.

I think that description captures so much of what people love about kirtan. What do you feel is the essence of the kirtan experience?

It's a downpour of love. I feel like there's light falling out of the sky. It's like a plant or a flower opening up to receive the rain. I feel like a thirsty plant. We're collecting together in one and receiving divine energy.

What is transpiring during a live kirtan performance for you and for the audience?

Each person has a connection or channel, a way of communicating with the divine. It's a vertical communication—me to God, spirit. When I do chanting I'm strengthening that connection. I'm walking that path over and over and over again to strengthen the connection to a presence, a presence of deities, a feeling of universal love. So when I do the chanting I'm doing it for myself. I'm trying to strengthen that connection.

During a kirtan, each person's connection is important. I do the kirtan for myself and I bring others along with me. You may not know how to get there yourself, but if you come along, then next time you know how to get there. I do my practice and bring along as many people as possible. My kirtan is an opening—a conversation between me and the audience. I'm trying to find out what they know, what commonalities we have so we can join together as a group.

Kirtan is different than chanting in a closet, which I did for fifteen years. That's not the gift that Krishna Das brings, to chant in a closet. The real beauty came when he went out in public. And I'd say the same for me.

What do you hope to help people understand through your kirtan?

I don't want people to understand! If you're drawn to do it, if you hear a CD and the mantra stays in your mind, then you want to know more. But I don't want to tell people that this is the way. There are a million ways. God is infinite. This is one way. If you're drawn to any aspect of it—the yoga, or the music, or the mantras, there's a lot of beauty there. I don't want to make sure anyone understands anything—I don't understand it! I'm just going to open up to experience whatever is there.

No experience needed. None is preferred.

Love is not serious. The energy that we're looking for—the lightness—is not heavy. When you're aligned with nature, things grow easily. Everything in nature is not serious. It's an expression of beauty. When you experience love, it's not analytical. It's fun. It carries a playful energy. If it comes from the head, I find the energy drops like a tank. If I'm just coming from my heart and sharing stories, the audience lightens and it turns into a more open experience. As we let go of our stuff, we open to a more loving state. We say it's the heart, but to be technical I think it's coming from the soul. But that sounds serious! It's joy, elation.

A unique thing about kirtan is that it's an individual experience happening within a group experience.

Doing it in a group is contagious. They say the energy doesn't just multiply, it grows exponentially. When joining together with other people, and you have one intention to open and expand to something greater than self, it's going to be powerful. Baptist churches, gatherings like Woodstock, that's the whole point–coming together with similar intention. Woodstock II didn't work because the intention was different.

One of the things I appreciate most about you is that you don't claim the spiritual journey is always a cakewalk. Searching can bring dissonance in your personal and professional life as your energy begins to change, as your vibration begins to move in a new direction. Many people are surprised at the chaos that can happen when they embark on spiritual self-exploration.

The nature of the light is to bring you to an experience of universality. Any issues you have, have to be brought out in the open, because these things get in the way, block the flow, block you from feeling love. As you strengthen your connection to the divine, all things that are not aligned with that become glaringly apparent and ask to be worked on. It feels like life is speeding up, because you can have more than one issue become glaringly apparent at one time.

Your lifestyle has to not be working in some sort of way to go to yoga or chanting in the first place—something has to fall apart and then you make a change. Something feels empty. And then you want to change your lifestyle. The karma, pain and suffering has to surface as you start these practices. All of a sudden things won't work right. These things don't come out in your practice, they come out in your life. That's when you need to run back to your practice to figure them out.

You wouldn't see these problems if you hadn't started ingesting large amounts of light. I won't see there's anything wrong with me, then I'll get around a saint, or a heavy tour schedule, and things start to fall apart. Many of us have some form of self-hatred; you have to look at it. The influx of light has changed it.

It starts purging things that you don't need, but didn't know you didn't need.

So it's sort of a Catch 22. Things are not working in your life so you start a practice, and then things might really not work! Most of us think it's all supposed to get better when we get on a spiritual path.

When you start purifying, you may wonder, "Is there something wrong with me? Where can I go for comfort?" I do workshops and kirtan to give us a chance to sit together, to feel this is the process. It's not that everything fell apart; you were holding onto things that were no longer integral to your path. It's part of the samskara—the suffering—that needs to be brought out. It gives perspective on how we hold onto things, hide things. As they come out, it's frightening.

That's the nature of purifying. Chanting is an influx of light. As we flow in the beauty and divine light and centeredness, the process starts. You can't just open your heart to receive love; you have to open to who you are.

You've done a lot of spiritual practices over the years.

For fifteen years I was doing japa (repeating a mantra) like crazy. I needed that austerity, that removal from society, living in the ashram in the late 70's, early 80's. I'm an intense person. I want an intense spiritual experience.

It's not about knowledge; it's about acquiring Self-knowledge. I spent fifteen years practicing a million techniques for meditation. I turned into a robot, became a perfect disciple. I was disciplined, but not more self-aware. After a while it turned out nobody was home. Those techniques didn't take me all the way, so now I need to take myself. Since I met Amma, it's become about bringing forward who I am, about understanding how precious being human, having an incarnation, is. Before it was about being a perfect person; now it's about using the practice to fill myself up and then share it with people. I use chanting, meditation, and yoga to connect with them.

Even when I'm with Amma, I still carry that austerity, which some people pick up on as coldness. Perhaps that's why my practice now focuses on creating that energy with other people—it softens me. I had a music teacher who once said, "Well, you're very good. But it sounds like you've been practicing alone in a closet. You've got to go out and play with people." What he said was about my music, but it was also a lot about me. It was time to stop the austerities and move into a more joyful practice.

And now I try to do it always: when I'm cooking, driving, in my friendships. I'm trying to apply that feeling of expanded Self in all aspects of my daily life. I take the belief that "God is in all" as a practice. I'm in a place of wondering if I can make it work. I have a longing to create that connection with whatever people are brought into my life.

Hopefully, whatever practice you have—be it Christian, Jewish, Hindu, yoga—hopefully, that will spill out into your life.

How you did you come to start singing kirtan?

I started doing musical mantras for my own benefit, just tapes for myself. People were digging it so I started making them for other people.

Some teachers advise people to silently recite the mantras in one's head. Others say chant them out loud.

Just the pitter patter of the tongue on the mouth, creating the vibration of those sounds, works. If you need to sing it, sing it. If you don't need to sing it, don't sing it. But manifest it!

What do you mean, "Manifest it?

I'm saying, "Make a noise!" Make your bones and your brain tissue and your muscles vibrate! Bring everything into manifestation, so you can see what it is. Because you won't know what it is unless it manifests. You won't know how screwed up you are until you screw up. And then you and your friends can go, "Damn. You really screwed up!" And you can see it and you go, "Oh, okay. So that's how it is." And then you can learn.

This is what it's all about for me now. Manifest it, bring it out. How many places can you manifest that amazing, joyous, spacious energy? And don't be selfish. Don't keep it all to yourself. Amma doesn't do that. All the people from the hotel (where Amma was just holding her program, leading kirtan and physically embracing everyone who came to see her) on their ten-minute break were taking off their shoes and coming in for a hug. Peter Jennings is coming in for a hug. The L.A. reporters who're there trying to get their news, they put that camera down before they leave and they go and get their hug. Amma doesn't see those boundaries and distinctions.

I think some people get so jazzed at kirtan because maybe they've never experienced that level of bliss before. What's exciting is that it's not about someone doing something to you or for you. It's about co-creating it.

Yeah, because they're singing too! The audience is creating their own connection. I'm not making their connection for them. Everybody's vertical and from that vertical connection, we're making a horizontal connection because we're sharing it together. But most of the time in our daily lives, the horizontal connection is the more predominant one. People talk to each other, they work together in their daily life. But most people don't come together and make this connection (Wah! motions from her heart to the sky).

Part of my focus in touring and traveling has been honoring the different ways people connect. We were on Long Island maybe six years ago, in what turned out to be a predominantly Buddhist community. But I didn't know that at the time. So I'm singing, "Sita Ram, Sita Ram" (the names of Hindu deities) and they're not singing anything back. (Wah! sings the mantra to demonstrate and then sits silently as if waiting for the response. Then she sings again, more tentatively, "Sita Ram, Sita Ram.")

Nothing! It made me really nervous. It was the first time that

I had sung and no one sang back. It was like, "I hope I'm not making you uncomfortable! Why don't we just have dinner?" (Wah! laughs at the memory.)

I sat there for my two hours and I did my thing, and talked and shared. Afterwards, every single CD we had brought to sell, was gone. They got so much out of it. They weren't comfortable with singing, because they never had before. They were very, very timid. Buddhists don't, or at that time anyway, weren't singing at all. And so this joyous, playful kind of practice was shocking to them. And yet we were able to honor each other's traditions and really share.

Kirtan is open to everybody. You've got healers, you've got drug addicts, you've got people who are doing yoga so they sit on the floor, and people who need to sit on chairs. There are people of all religions. Kirtan isn't a group you have to join. It's just an experience that you can share. It is open to everybody, and that gives me a chance to connect with a lot of different kinds of people, to share a lot of different traditions and healing practices. And there's something very fulfilling about that.

Everything about the kirtan changed me. It's been quite a ride. I don't think anyone expects the transformation when they start chanting.

We're so open at the end of kirtan. Do we really need to close down to go back into our life? The goal is to stay open while still honoring our responsibilities. I believe the way we feel after kirtan is the standard. The job is to raise the vibe in the rest of your life.

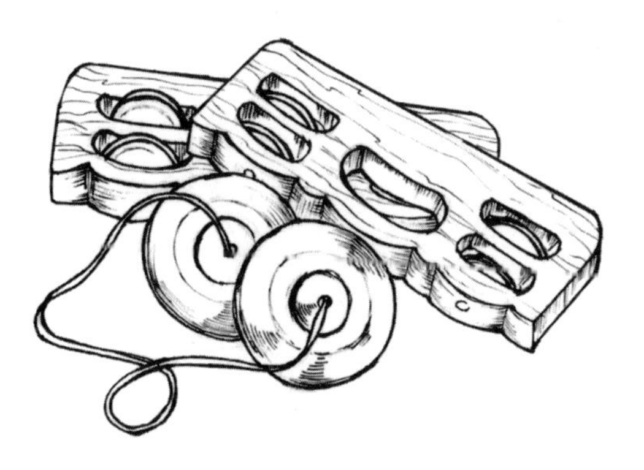

Joining In

The simplest way to begin a kirtan practice is to start singing! It's really that easy. Attend a local kirtan or order a few kirtan CDs so you can learn some chants, and you're good to go. The websites of the artists profiled in this book are listed at the end of this chapter, along with other helpful resources to help you find the best chant music.

Kirtan is set to myriad musical genres—classical Indian, rock-n-roll, jazz, reggae, Gospel, fusion, and more. It's important to select a musical style and artist you resonate with. Many Internet-based CD sales sites allow you to listen to clips of a CD before purchasing it. You can also stop in at a local yoga studio or New Age bookstore and ask for suggestions.

Ready to sing? As with most spiritual practices, it's helpful to create an environment conducive to the experience. Here are some tips:

• Choose a place that's quiet, where you won't be interrupted. Find a space that allows you to let go of any inhibitions you might have about singing, especially about singing loudly. Being able to chant with abandon, with full passion, is part of the joy of kirtan.

• Sit comfortably. Traditionally kirtan is practiced sitting on the floor, but chairs are fine too. Be sure to sit up straight, which allows your breath and energy to flow fully.

• It may be helpful to dim the lights and close your eyes to minimize distractions and allow the sound to permeate your awareness.

• Turn on the music and open your heart!

Like any spiritual practice, setting time aside each day, preferably at the same time if possible, makes it a true practice. But if you find that difficult to manage, weekly or monthly sessions will also enhance your spiritual life.

Try replacing some of the music you usually listen to with kirtan. Surrounding yourself with a sacred vibrations is always beneficial. Some people listen to kirtan nearly twenty-four hours a day, even as they fall asleep!

Live Kirtan

Kirtan is exponentially more powerful when practiced with others. If there is not a live kirtan available in your community, try inviting friends to join you in singing to a CD. You'll be amazed at the power of your combined voices even when singing to a recording!

To find out if there is live kirtan in your area, check with local yoga studios or search online by typing in the name of your city and the word "kirtan." When attending a kirtan, it's often a good idea to bring a pillow or cushion if you plan to sit on the floor; not every venue has enough cushions.

Don't be afraid to sing with gusto. The more each of us lets go, the more it gives others the confidence to do the same. The more energy we put into the kirtan, the more we—and the entire group—receive. Never mind if you can't carry a tune: no one can hear you in the crowd. In fact, often you can't even hear yourself! One of the many magical gifts of kirtan is that, regardless of the quality of each individual voice, the resulting mix is heavenly. We all walk out of an evening of chanting feeling like the Mariah Carey of kirtan.

Some traditions suggest you remain seated during the kirtan so that the energy can flow directly up the spine as the mantras weave their meditative web. Others encourage you to dance yourself into bliss. Each crowd is different as well. Do what feels most natural for you.

Here's another important way in which kirtan differs from a concert. At the end of each chant, no matter how sublimely the musicians played, there is no applause. The room sits in silence, often for several minutes, soaking up the energy.

The beauty of kirtan is its effortlessness. It automatically lifts your soul to a whole new dimension of spiritual experience. No wonder the great yoga master Swami Sivananda said, "Chanting is the easiest of all ways to approach God."

RESOURCES

Getting Started

Is there a kirtan group in your community? Will a favorite kirtan artist be visiting your area soon? Would you like to advertise your own kirtan program? What are some of the best new kirtan CDs? Want to chant with others who have similar tastes in music? This website, sponsored by the International Kirtan Foundation, is an invaluable resource for both kirtan leaders and participants:

www.KirtanConnection.com

Here is the website for the largest seller of independent music on the Internet:

www.CDbaby.com

The Artists

Want to learn more about the kirtan artists profiled in this book? Interested in picking up their latest recordings? Here are their websites:

www.KrishnaDas.com
www.DevaPremal.com
www.BhagavanDas.com
www.SnatamKaur.com
www.RaganiWorld.com
www.JaiUttal.com
www.DaveStringer.com
www.WahMusic.com

Paramahansa Yogananda, one of the first yoga masters to teach in America, loved to lead kirtan. He assured his students that music is a divine art that can be used as a path to God realization. "In Thy temple of the Earth, in a chorus of many-accented voices," he wrote, "we are singing only to Thee."

Like the medieval choirs of angels, let's all join our many-accented voices in joy!

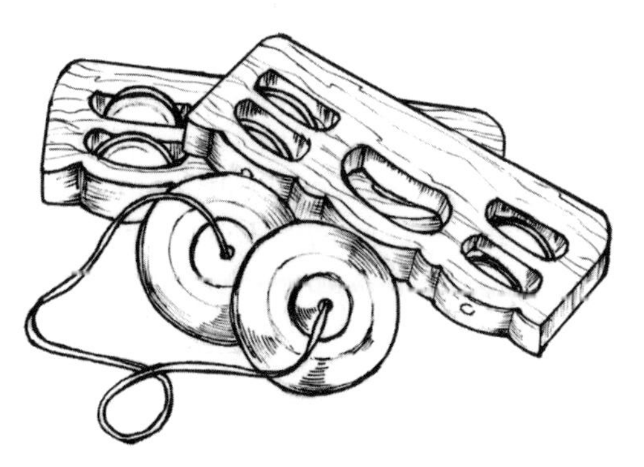

Holy Names

The mantras we sing in kirtan are usually either Sanskrit names for God or words describing his wonderful qualities. They have been chanted so many trillions of times that the very sound of the syllables resonates with the intense devotion of centuries of heart-felt worship. You don't need to know what the words mean to feel their amazing transformative power.

Some people, though, are curious about the hidden significance of the mantras and want to expand their practice of kirtan by connecting more deeply with the beautiful divine names. They also wonder why people in India use so many different names for God.

Just as Christians worship three gods-in-one (Father, Son, and Holy Spirit), Indians worship thirty-three billion gods-in-one. The *Rig Veda*, the oldest and most sacred scripture of India, says, "There is one God. Men call him by different names." People there believe that as long as you call out to him sincerely, the Supreme Being responds to your prayer, no matter what name you use for him.

It doesn't matter what religion you belong to, or whether you picture God as male or female, as human-looking or as a transcendent spirit. Every creature in the universe is his child and he loves us all equally. Therefore every name for God in any language is equally valid. Even if there are thirty-three billion of them!

In the ancient Middle East there were numerous names for God which all came from a similar root—these included "Allah" in Arabic (used by both Arabic-speaking Christians and Muslims), "Allaha" in Aramaic, "Elohim" in old Hebrew, and "Elat" in the language of the pre-Canaanites. This holy name appears in the *Rig Veda* too, where it was pronounced "Ila." Though different, these names for God are also all the same.

Remember, the word "God" was never used in the original manuscripts of the Bible, Torah or Koran. "God" was a pagan European word for "deity," and was often used for the Norse god Odin. The ancient Egyptians used to chant the divine name Amun at the end of their hymns, which is where we got our word "Amen." We wouldn't stop adding "Amen" to our prayers just because it's a divine name in another language!

Here is a short glossary of the divine names most commonly used in kirtan. We've also included a few North Indian words (in italics) that you'll often hear in the bhajans. We hope these explanations enhance your appreciation of the joyous and loving spirit of kirtan!

Amba	The Divine Mother.
Amma	Same as "Amba."
Atma	The all-pervading divine spirit at the center of our being.
bhajan	A devotional song.
bolo	"Sing!"
Brahma	Creator of the universe.
Devaki	The mother of Krishna, whose extreme delight at the birth of her son represents our great joy when God becomes a living presence in our lives.
Devi	Goddess.

Durga	The Goddess as a warrioress who fiercely protects her children. She's often shown sitting on a lion.
Ganapati	Same as "Ganesha."
Ganesha	The divine being who clears away obstacles to the fulfillment of our worthy desires. He's shown with an elephant head to indicate his indomitable strength.
Gayatri	The Goddess as the mother of sacred wisdom. The Gayatri mantra means, "With loving reverence, we bow to the divine inner Sun, the most splendid light in all the worlds. Please illuminate our awareness!"
Gopala	God in the form of a young cow-herder. Metaphorically, we humans are the cows he guides and protects.
Govinda	Same as "Gopala."
Hanuman	A perfect devotee who devoted his life to serving Rama (God) He is visualized in the form of monkey to suggest the speed and enthusiasm of his selfless service. He represents our "monkey mind" when it's put to the best possible use.
Hara, Hare, Hari	These are three related words all meaning lord, protector, or enchanter of hearts.
jai	"Hail!"
jaya	"Hail!"
Kali	The Goddess as the destroyer of evil, and of everything less than divine in ourselves.
Krishna	God pictured as a playful cow-herder, a divine lover, a prince, and a sage. His timeless words of spiritual advice are preserved for us in the Bhagavad Gita.
Lakshmi	The Goddess as bestower of prosperity, good fortune and well being.
Mahadeva	Same as "Shiva."
namah	"I offer my loving respect."
namo	Same as "namah."
Om	According to yogis, this most sacred of all mantras is the first sound God uttered when he broke his perfect silence and manifested the universe.

Parvati	The Goddess pictured as a female yogi.
Radha	A milk-maid who was the love-intoxicated girlfriend of Krishna. She represents the devotee who has completely lost herself in ecstatic yearning for God.
Rama	God pictured as the perfect king and husband. A famous Indian epic called the *Ramayana* chronicles his adventures. Rama's passionate love for his wife Sita is an allegory for God's love for each human soul.
Sarasvati	The Goddess of wisdom, education, and the arts, especially music.
Shankara	Same as "Shiva."
shanti	Peace.
Shiva	God in the form of a wild mystic who wanders the mountains and sits for eons in meditation. He is also the divine dancer who dissolves the universe into himself at the end of time.
Sita	The perfect wife. Sita's absolute commitment to her husband Rama is an allegory for the devotee's all-encompassing love for God.
Siva	Another spelling for Shiva.
Vasudeva	Same as "Vishnu"; also Krishna's father.
Vishnu	The protector of the universe. Rama and Krishna were great heroes who embodied Vishnu's wisdom, compassion, and strength in human form.
wallah	A person who performs a specific type of service such as a *dobi wallah* (laundry man) or *kirtan wallah* (kirtan singer or musician).

The Authors

Maggie Jacobus has spent years delving into the transforming power of sacred sound. In this book she shares her avid research, study and practice of kirtan. A certified sound healer, singer in a kirtan band, and a founding board member of the International Kirtan Foundation, Maggie is also the author of more than 75 magazine and newspaper articles on alternative health and wellness. She is a contributing reporter for *The New York Times* and is the executive producer of a children's nature program. You can visit her at www.MaggieJacobus.com.

Linda Johnsen is a contributing editor for *Yoga International, Yoga+*, and *The Mountain Astrologer.* She has written several articles for Himalayan Path, Yoga Journal, and other magazines. Among her many books are *Daughters of the Goddess: The Women Saints of India, The Living Goddess,* and *The Complete Idiot's Guide to Hinduism.* An ardent kirtan enthusiast, Linda considers sacred chant a highway to higher states of consciousness. You'll find her website at www.ThousandSuns.org.

Acknowledgments

I am in deepest gratitude to my husband, Steve, and my three boys—Ryan, Michael and William—for supporting me in my sacred sound quest and the writing of this book; to my Sister-in-Dreams and kirtan bliss, Ragani; to Jai Uttal, Dave Stringer, and Wah! for sharing their stories and their music with me; to Gurushabd for all his eloquent insights; and to the sages who translated for us all the divine songs of the universe. —*Maggie Jacobus*

Thanks so much to my good friend and neighbor, Bette Timm, the calm center of the kirtan cyclone, for smoothing my path to the artists; to my husband, Johnathan Brown, who cheerfully juggled the recording equipment and digital cameras while I conducted the interviews; to Krishna Das, Bhagavan Das, Deva Premal, Snatam Kaur, and my guru-sister Ragani, for graciously answering my long lists of questions; and to kirtan wallahs everywhere for creating the music that makes Earth feel like Heaven.

—*Linda Johnsen*

Maggie and Linda would both like to extend their special gratitude to Ma Devi and the staff at Yes International Publishers for helping bring the story of the yoga chant movement and eight of its greatest artists to kirtan addicts everywhere!

Books from Yes International Publishers